The Essential Inheritance of the

# LONDON
# CONTEMPORARY
# DANCE
# THEATRE

The Essential Inheritance of the

# LONDON
# CONTEMPORARY
# DANCE
# THEATRE

Edited by Ross McKim

DANCE
BOOKS

Published by Dance Books Ltd, The Old Bakery,
4 Lenten Street, Alton, Hampshire GU34 1HG
www.dancebooks.co.uk

This book was originally published by Harwood Academic Press,
Taylor & Francis Ltd., http://www.tandf.co.uk/journals, as volume 6
part 4 in the series *Choreography and Dance*

ISBN 185273 101 X

Production by Liz Morrell & Patrick Donnelly
Printed by Russell Press, Nottingham, UK

# Contents

# Foreword: Something of the History of the London Contemporary Dance Theatre

Ross McKim

## Chronology

**1954**   Robin Howard sees the Martha Graham company.

**1963**   Howard enables British dancers to study with Graham in New York.

**1966**   Howard founds the Contemporary Dance Trust.

**1967**   Robert Cohan appointed Director of the Trust.

**1967**   London School of Contemporary Dance founded.

**1969**   The Trust moves to The Place.

**1972**   First Sadlers Wells season (the move to larger theatres).

**1976**   First "residencies" in Yorkshire.

**1979**   The Place doubles in size.

**1982**   School becomes based on degree work.

**1989**   Howard dismissed from the Board of the Trust.

**1990**   Robin Howard dies.

**1994**   Arts Council funding is withdrawn – the company closes.

Robin Howard, the man who formed what was to become the London Contemporary Dance Theatre, was the son of Sir Arthur Howard a member of Parliament; Stanley Baldwin was his grandfather. He served as a Lieutenant in the Scots Guards in World War II. During this service he sustained war wounds that resulted in the loss of his legs. Although he later studied law and was called to the Bar he did not practice. In about 1972, at his house in Sandwich Street in London, he showed me books of press clippings concerning Ballet that led me to believe he could once have been called a balletomane.

In 1954, in London, Howard first saw the Martha Graham company perform and was deeply impressed. Discovering that the Graham company was to visit Europe in 1962, but would not come to the UK, Howard set out to alter this situation. Through marshalling the support of Francis Mason of the American Embassy, Clive Barnes, the dance critic for the London Times, and Lord Harewood, director of the Edinburgh

**Figure 1**
**Robin Howard. Photo: Anthony Crickmay. Courtesy of V&A Picture Library.**

Festival, and pledging a substantial sum of his own money, he did much to bring the company to Edinburgh and London in 1963.[1]

Howard then set up a Trust (which he at first called the Contemporary Ballet Trust) which began by bringing dancers from the Graham company to London to give classes. This, in 1966, led to the formation of the London School of Contemporary Dance. The principal technique studied was derived from Martha Graham, but even then Ballet and choreographic composition were also taught. In 1967, at Howard's request, Robert Cohan came to London as artistic director of the Trust, having agreed to take on responsibility for its development.[2] In the same year the London Contemporary Dance Group gave its first performances. The structure of the company as evident in this performance was to characterize it for some time. It was made up of stars from the Graham company (in this case Noemi Lapzeson and Robert Powell) supported by students of the school. Performances by the Group followed around the country in schools, colleges, universities and community halls.

In 1968 the Trust re-organized the school so that it could offer a full-time three-year course. Then, in 1969, the now London Contemporary Dance Theatre (LCDT) gave its first performances in its own theatre within its own building, "The Place," for which Howard had recently acquired the lease. This building was to house the school, the company and its administrative back-up. Howard also planned it as a multi-purpose arts center that could support experiment in dance and other art forms. Cohan now decided to devote himself full time to Howard's venture.

The next decade would probably be judged a period of great artistic success by most who followed the life of the LCDT. Some would cite this successful period as lasting for a good deal longer. The company became self-sufficient in terms of its dancers and in its choreography. Gradually the stars of the Graham company gave way to dancers trained in the school. Cohan, Siobhan Davies, Robert North, Micha Bergese and then others provided most of the choreography. The company moved from small-scale theatres and halls to middle theatres particularly with the first highly successful Sadlers Wells Theatre season in 1973. Large-scale theatre touring began in 1979. International touring rendered further success. There was critical and audience acclaim and significant financial support.

There was much that was unusual and so perhaps of particular interest in the LCDT's success. This was a company forging its way in a UK where very little Modern or Contemporary Dance had been seen before. It was doing so on the basis of dancers it trained or retrained through an on-going development of the Graham Technique, very largely on the basis of Cohan's creative initiative, which many would argue was unique and important.[3] The works on which the excitement of the company was based were made by artists of the company who were finding their choreographic voice through its development.[4] Even Cohan was not a very well-known choreographer before this period; he became one through it. All in all, during this time, the company entered the ranks of what tend to be called the "best" international companies both in terms of its dancers and in terms of the original works.

Arguably, however, in spite of its early success, the problems that were to kill the company began to emerge very early. Significantly Robin Howard wrote, "I do not hesitate to say that until 1976, I loved every minute of my work for the Trust. Since that date, I have increasingly disliked the way in which I have had to spend my time." (Clarke & Crisp, 1987: 190). This statement of Howard's is perhaps evidence that even in 1976 the company was beginning to become caught up in certain artistic problems which, as discussed in this issue, led to its demise. The artistic success of the company seemed to be becoming forced to depend on a system of income generation that would eventually destroy it.

Finally, with Howard and Cohan no longer involved, the management

**Figure 2**
**Robert Cohan. Photo: Anthony Crickmay. Courtesy of V&A Picture Library.**

of the company gave up trying to keep it alive. "Two weeks before
LCDT's season at Sadlers Wells (November 23–December 4 1993) the
Board of the LCDT told its dancers the company had no future. The
Board had been unable to agree on an artistic director or a future policy
which it believed the Arts Council would accept" (Parry, 1994).

In the end it is perhaps the case that "Cohan's withdrawal from the
directorship of the LCDT was eventually, after more than twenty years,

inevitable.[5] He was exhausted, having been asked to do too much" (Drummond, 1996). His success and that of his LCDT, however, seem more important and more worthy of memory than any failure. The legacy of Cohan's work, which Howard made possible, might usefully be brought to mind and studied. This would particularly appear to be so since many of those who worked with him believe that "He has taught us all lessons about integrity and standards in life as well as in dance. Today, when so much second-rate posturing passes as innovation, he is here to remind us that dance can be much more than trivial entertainment, and artistic direction more than a passive pose" (Drummond, 1996: 12).

## References

Clarke, M. & Crisp, C. (1987) *The London Contemporary Dance Theatre*. London: Dance Books.
Drummond, J. (1996) A golden stage. *Dance Theatre Journal*, 13, 10–12.
Parry, J. (1994) London Contemporary Dance Theatre. *Dancing Times*, 84, 338–339.

## Notes

1. Howard spent his own money on aspects of the Contemporary Dance Trust for as long as he was involved with it.
2. Cohan's plan was to spend half his time in London and half in New York with the Graham company.
3. In 1976, the term Graham Technique was dropped in referring to the work of the school.
4. Richard Alston, who choreographed a great deal for the company, was not one of its dancers. None the less, calling him "of" the organization seems fair. He was one of the first students of the school and later taught composition there. The company was his chief choreographic outlet until he formed *Strider* in 1972 and he choreographed regularly for it until well after that date.
5. There had been attempts to replace Cohan by a worthy successor but none had succeeded.

# Introduction: Concerning What the London Contemporary Dance Theatre Inherited

Ross McKim

## Meaning and the Spiritual in Dance

The Modern Dance that Robin Howard brought to the UK, and which flourished within the London Contemporary Dance Theatre (LCDT), was of a serious-minded tradition. Many modern dance artists thought along the lines of Wassily Kandinsky, whose *Concerning The Spiritual In Art* was published in 1911 as modern dance was beginning to develop.[1] He wrote of "the internal truth which only art can divine, which only art can express by those means of expression which are her's alone" (Kandinsky, 1977 [1911]: 9). Kandinsky said artists will be the spiritual leaders of the future. He spoke of "this new spirit . . . going hand in hand with the spirit of thought towards an epoch of great spiritual leaders" (Kandinsky, 1977 [1911]: 57). Modern dancers and Robin Howard appeared to subscribe to a movement, not limited to the arts, that sought to provide a sense of "meaning" in a most significant sense.

It can be argued that this movement was dealing with the effects of the crisis of religious belief of the nineteenth century. "God is dead. God remains dead. And we have killed him," (Neitzsche, 1985 [1883]: 125) cried Neitzsche's mad man. Western religion, for many, ceased to provide a final sense of the meaning. This generated a powerfully creative compensatory urge not limited to the arts. In philosophy, Wittgenstein spoke of the meaning in things that "cannot be put into words . . . [but] make themselves manifest [and] are what is mystical" (Wittgenstein, 1961 [1921]: 73). Einstein spoke of the need for experience that provided a "depth of the conviction concerning its overpowering meaningfulness . . ." (Einstein, 1950: 25). The quest seemed particularly energized in the 1960s and 1970s when the LCDT flourished. About that time Jerzy Grotowski began to pursue theatre centering on "the holy actor."

1

## Places of Change

Rudolf Von Laban wrote of Central European Modern Dance rather than the American variety out of which the London Contemporary Dance Theatre grew. He clarified a theory of purpose, however, probably held by many of the most significant modern dance artists in differing forms and at differing levels of consciousness or unconsciousness. Dance's "purpose" is "to create a life . . . filled with a spiritual attitude . . ." (Laban, 1975 [1935]: 84). Performances should possess "the character and form of the sacred act" (Laban, 1975 [1935]: 88). Through these the dancer "perceives another, entirely different, world" (Laban, 1975 [1935]: 90).

The dancers' experience and knowledge of "an energy behind all occurrences and material things" (Laban, 1975 [1935]: 90) are beyond rational comprehension. "Oneness," the endpoint of much religious experience, is available through dance. This is oneness with "the universal soul out of which and for which we have to create" (Laban, 1975 [1935]: 94).

Dancers are a special group of people through the unique experience dance renders to them. The dancer's experience is more significant than that of witnesses who "can but get a taste of this vital nourishment through the enjoyment they derive from artistic works of dance" (Laban, 1975 [1935]: 90). The superiority of the experience of the artist perhaps relates to the "fallen" state of most art. Laban will prepare his performers but he cannot so prepare audiences. But Laban may also imply that, like religious seers, artists see more deeply into the nature of things than those to whom they communicate their vision.

The legacy of a dance form may pass down through its "technique" as much as through its choreographed works. Laban did not supply a technique. He does not say what kind of dance generates the special experience of which he speaks and so implies all dance does, which is probably not true. His disciple Mary Wigman took the next logical step as did other modern dance creators. Since only some dance generates special experience this dance must be sought. To have the ability to do this dance is to possess the "technique" to do so. So Wigman "plunged into work on a dance technique, a notion which then did not yet exist for the new free-style dance. Laban did not show much interest in it" (Wigman, 1975: 52).

Wigman's search revealed what dance needed to be done and how to do it. Her principal aim, following Laban's line but with a greater expressionist emphasis appears to have been "ecstatic" experience and "intoxication," not only or mainly the acquisition of skills. She, like Laban, speaks of attaining knowledge of oneness. She does so through a technique.

**Figure 3**
**Robert Cohan, Bob Smith, Paula Lansley. Photo: Anthony Crickmay.**
**Courtesy of V&A Picture Library.**

I gave myself up to the intoxication of this experience . . . a process in which, for seconds, I almost felt oneness with the cosmos. I turned and turned until I succeeded in tracing its secret . . . to bring these turns back into the sphere of their ecstatic experience. (Wigman, 1975: 52)

What Wigman calls ecstasy provides experience that appears to be a kind of knowledge; special experience of this kind is reported by American modern dancers also. Isadora Duncan wrote of special experience which can become its own expression. As part of her dance technique she devised a method to generate and utilize this.

I had learned to concentrate all my force to this one Centre . . . when I listened to music the rays and vibrations of the music streamed to this one fount of light within me – there they reflected themselves in Spiritual Vision . . . and from this vision I could express them in Dance. (Duncan, 1988 [1928]: 59)

Duncan said her special experience would supply "a renaissance of religion through Dance" (Duncan, 1988 [1928]: 65).

Ruth St Denis was a Christian Scientist. "By instinct and inheritance she was a mystic . . ." (Shelton, 1981: 3). She says that through dance "I am near reality and in a more harmonious state of being than at any other time. I find a real escape from the limited sense of life. . . . Human relationships are suspended and the sense of age" (St Denis, cited in Shelton, 1981: 206).

For Martha Graham, the quasi-religious experience of the dancer was related to that available through depth psychology. In the 1920s she knew of Freud for whom experience of the psyche was important knowledge (De Mille, 1992: 250). Then, in the early 1940s, through people like her husband Eric Hawkins, her designer Isamu Nogouchi and the mythologist Joseph Campbell (who married one of her dancers) she learned of Jung's thought. This included his understanding of the deep experience of the psyche as religious experience or, as he put it, "the experience of God". She used the religious function of psychology, as explicated by Jung, to contribute to the religious function of dance (De Mille, 1992: 250).

Graham was also a close friend of "Mrs. Wicks, the lay analyst and writer who had been Jung's mistress and who was a devout apostle of the master" (De Mille, 1992: 279). De Mille claimed that Jungian theory, in combination with that of kundalini ". . . seemed to bring enlightenment to Martha" (De Mille, 1992: 250).[2] Graham's Technique appears to seek profound experience not just to develop skills. Many exercises, particularly on the floor, bore relation to the Tantric thought which underlies Hatha Yoga (Lang, cited in De Mille, 1991: 251). Graham's dance training, at least in part, is thus comparable to a spiritual training in which profound experience and knowledge is the goal.

Robert Cohan, and the dance technique of his London Contemporary Dance Theatre, were influenced by Graham. He danced with Graham from 1946 to 1967. His concerns were closely related to hers and centered on experience of the "inner landscape." The dancer comes to know and then "to illustrate and project the inner world of man's experience by direct physical action in space" (Cohan, 1986: 150). Like Graham, Cohan's class exercises had more than physical purpose. For him dance "exercises the whole being" (Cohan, 1986: 10).

Like Graham he saw this as taking place through quasi-religious confrontation with the self as in Jungian analysis. "As you try to improve your body's movements, you will collide head-on with your emotions – which may have been in control of your body until now" (Cohan, 1986: 14). The event of the "class" becomes "a ritual . . . in order to find yourself you need to go through the ritual form" (Cohan, 1986: 1).

Outer physical changes that arise through dance training are symptoms of something more significant. Cohan says, "for me the training . . . has always been like a form of Yoga. The outer changes were only symptoms of that inner discipline" (Cohan, cited in Gow, 1972: 187).

Although Cohan and Graham tended not so bluntly to claim religious status as had early modern dancers, Cohan says,

She [Graham] is an extremely religious person in a way . . . she had a great sense of what is holy about life and that influenced me a great deal. Outside of that I looked for my own ideas of what is sacred in life. (Cohan cited in Gow, 1972: 187)

So it appears that the London Contemporary Dance Theatre of Robin Howard and Robert Cohan searched for a special kind of meaning in life through art, a meaning that would once have been called "sacred." This meaning was to emerge out of the experience of dancing. It could be called "metaphysical meaning" or indeed "metalogical meaning" because it is beyond logical processes and logical experience. Even though it is attained through dance it is also beyond ordinary physical experience.

Cohan's concern for experience and knowledge that give a sense of such meaning is evident in the titles and contents of his works: *Hunter Of Angels* deals with a Jungian confrontation with aspects of the inner self, which must be overcome; *X* and *Cell* are psychological studies of people who can find, or build, no meaning into their lives; *Stages* is about the quest of a Ulysses-like hero; and the central solo of *Khamsin* appears to be about someone who searches for meaning he does not find; *Masque of Separation* was originally called *Myth*. Cohan told us (the members of his company) that he began by reading myths and then wrote his own. He used other mythic material like that of Orpheus and Euridice in *No Man's Land* and he used Christian mythic material in *Mass* and *Stabat Mater*. The function he saw as that of the LCDT is perhaps best stated in the title of his work *Place Of Change*.

Laban, Wigman, Duncan, St Denis, Graham and Cohan were or are unusual people and worked in dance partly because this was so. They were also of a particularly creative period that perhaps allowed a certain artistic attitude. Their search for a special kind of meaning is no more evident in all present contemporary dance than it is in most contemporary life.

## The Process, Product Equivalence and their Purpose

As a member of the LCDT between 1970 and 1976, I was made aware of Robert Cohan's attitude. I never heard him use the word "spiritual", not when dancing in his company nor later when teaching in his school, nor when speaking and travelling with him, or in interviewing him. It is a difficult word and perhaps prejudicial if you deal in a physical art form.[3] Like Grotowski however, he seemed to feel there was something "holy" to be attained through performing and preparation for performance.

As shown in his following interview, he appeared concerned in class,

**Figure 4**
Robert Cohan rehearsing *Shanta*. Choreography, Siobhan Davies.
Photo: Anthony Crickmay. Courtesy of V&A Picture Library.

rehearsal, performance and the activities that surround these, with "inner" transformation. At least some of us in his company understood he meant that this must take place in us, largely through studio work, before it could be evident in performance. He may have placed more importance on inner change than Graham. I think part of him disliked the "showy" part of a show.

The view that the experience of process (pre-performance work) is as important as product (performance) existed in much of the modern dance tradition. The quotations above, from or concerning Laban, Wigman, Duncan, St Denis and Graham are evidence of this. The process has the objective of making product but it is also product in itself. Indeed class, rehearsal and performance can all have a purpose beyond themselves and beyond theatrical success in the conventional sense. This was Grotowski's attitude.

The theatre, he (Grotowski) believes cannot be an end in itself; like dancing or music in certain dervish orders, the theatre is a vehicle, a means of self-study, a possibility of salvation. (Brook, 1984 [1968]: 67)

Cohan's "company class" was not like that of most Ballet and Contemporary companies today. For many years he taught this himself. It was not a warm-up or solely physical training session of an hour or hour and a quarter. It was scheduled for an hour and a half and very often ran overtime to an hour and three-quarters or more. His "experimentation" was deeply worked and within a consistent area probably for the same reason as Grotowski's was. It appeared that both men did not wish their work to be "tangential (toying with some 'new' technique each time) and tributary" (Grotowski, 1981 [1968]: 15).

The eclectic use of many different teachers for daily classes, to provide "richness" or to keep the dancers from becoming bored was not followed. Eclecticism in performance method and technique can provide "the 'Rich Theatre' – rich in flaws. . . . Consequently I propose poverty in theatre" (Grotowski, 1981 [1968]: 15). Cohan, like Grotowski, saw to it that the studio work of his company was consistent, serious, deep and probing in the sense that depth psychology and religious exercises can be.

This attitude towards the "mundane work" of the studio appeared to be based, in modern dance and in Grotowski's early theatre, on the notion that the performer must be capable of profound experience to express it and so make that experience, or some part of it, available to the witness of performance. This experience, although it arose in performance, depended largely on transformative work that took place outside it.

**Figure 5**
**Robert Cohan, Namron, Derick Linton. Photo: Anthony Crickmay.**
**Courtesy of V&A Picture Library.**

## Legacy, Loss and Finding

It is easy to point to direct elements of the legacy of the LCDT through people. Siobhan Davies and Richard Alston head two of the major Contemporary Dance companies in the UK. Robert North continues to choreograph with major companies around the world. Anthony Van Laast and Micha Bergese have been influential in the commercial dance scene. Several major teaching establishments are or have been headed by former LCDT people: Middlesex University Dance School by Christopher Bannerman and Rambert School, which advertises its contemporary work as "Robert Cohan-based" by myself. Professor Bannerman continues to teach on MA programmes at Middlesex and leads a research centre there. There are people from various generations of the company influencing young dancers through their choreography. Perhaps more often such influence is transmitted through teaching posts by way of which it can be consistent and thorough. The London Contemporary Dance School remains a powerful force. The Northern School Of Contemporary Dance, set up with the LSCD as a model, is thriving. The Contemporary Dance Trust also continues through its evening school and other activities.

Yet none of this is conclusive evidence that the essential inheritance of the LCDT has survived. It is possible, however, that if it has not it could be rediscovered. This issue might help towards this.

## References

Brook, P. (1984 [1968]) *The Empty Space*. London: Pelican.

Cohan, R. (1986) *The Dance Workshop*. London: Unwin.

De Mille, A. (1992) *Martha*. New York: Vintage Books.

Duncan, I. (1968 [1928]) *My Life*. London: Sphere Books.

Einstein, A. (1950) *Out of My Later Years*. New York: Philosophical Library.

Gow, G. (1972) Cohan and Contemporary Dance. *Dancing Times,* January, 186–187.

Grotowski, J. (1981 [1964]) *Towards a Poor Theatre*. London: Methuen.

Laban, R. (1975 [1935]) *A Life for Dance*. London: MacDonald and Evans.

Neitzsche, F. (1969) *Thus Spoke Zarathustra*. London: Penguin.

Shelton, S. (1981) *Divine Dancer*. New York, Doubleday.

Wigman, M. (1966) *The Language of Dance*. Middlestown, Connecticut: Wesley University Press.

Wittgenstein, L.(1974 [1921]) *Tractatus Logico-Philosophicus*. London: Routledge and Kegan Paul.

## Notes

1. By modern dance is meant here a set of styles emerging from the beginning of the twentieth century, within the tradition of Western theatrical dance, which often largely rejected ballet. Following this characterization of the term, Ruth St Denis was a modern dancer who is generally thought to have significantly influenced Martha Graham. St Denis produced her famous solo work *Radha* in 1906.

2. Kundalini Yoga deals with causing or allowing the potentially spiritual energy, that is believed to reside at the base of the spine, to rise. This energy thus passes through seven psychological centers called *padmas* (lotuses) or *chakras* (wheels) which are located along the spine. As this spiritual energy reaches each centre a transformation of consciousness takes place.

3. I say this because the spiritual tends to be thought the opposite of the physical at least in the West.

# Transformative Dance: An Interview with Christopher Bannerman

Ross McKim

At: Middlesex University
On: 22 July 1998

RM: Has there been an influence or effect on the UK dance scene now from the London Contemporary Dance Theatre?

CB: You are asking someone who was a member of that company for almost fifteen years and so there was clearly an effect on me. At the material level the company paid my wages; however, I assume that is not the level of this discussion. My assessment of the dance world is that the LCDT exerted a significant influence for a number of years.

RM: Would the UK dance scene have been better or worse off had there not been this influence?

CB: Making that assessment would be very difficult and I don't think I would attempt it. In trying to assess what might have happened if the LCDT had not arrived, we are dealing with something that is hypothetical and therefore does not stand academic scrutiny, unless one is working with theories of what hasn't happened. In my view it would be a useless exercise to speculate in this way; however, by the time the LCDT ceased to exist, there was a flourishing of dance activity; I do not think it is too tenuous to say that the company had influenced at least some of that development. Some of the people and things which emerged from and with the company are still influential and active today. All of these have to be seen as contributors to our understanding of dance, the arts and culture in Britain today.

RM: The LCDT was criticized by English academics and English critics as an artificial American import that did not represent artistic needs here.

CB: It may be a sadness to some people that all this came from America and represented a strong American influence. I suppose that this sentiment has to be seen in the wider context of American cultural influence on

11

**Figure 6**
Chistopher Bannerman, Celia Hulton in *Ceremony*. Choreography, Robert Cohan.
Photo: Anthony Crickmay. Courtesy of V&A Picture Library.

Britain and indeed on the rest of the world. However, that influence is an historical fact and that does not diminish the reality of the dance world here today, which I believe has established a British identity.

RM: There was American Modern Dance and Central European Modern Dance. The latter was largely destroyed by the war so American Modern Dance was principally what there was to draw on. American Modern Dance entered the UK through teachers like Clover Roope and choreographers like Glenn Tetley at Rambert and through the LCDT. Do you think the dance that began as American Modern Dance became something else through the processes of the LCDT, or do you think the dance the LCDT left behind had something in it American Modern Dance did not?

CB: I should say that I will answer the question in relation to what I will term "Contemporary Dance" as I think this term denotes a British form. To call the form "Modern Dance" is to adopt the model of another country. While I understand the issues about "Modernism" in an academic sense, none the less we are all, academics included, located in Britain, and Contemporary Dance has assumed a legitimacy in this context.

Secondly, I believe that the influence of the LCDT, like that of Laban, is currently being re-evaluated; this is simply because of the new perspective that the passage of time is allowing. Previously the evaluation was coloured by our proximity to events. There is a question about what distance in time is appropriate for these things and I have a sympathy with the view that the former Chinese Premier, Chou En-lai, allegedly expressed about the French revolution: it's too soon to tell!

RM: One thing that might be of value, in asking if there is influence of the LCDT on dance now, is to find what is valuable in what is left, what can be picked out and built upon.

CB: Yes, I didn't really take the "now" part of your first question fully on board. I suppose that if the LCDT had an influence on the past and the past continues to influence the present, then arguably there is still some influence present today. I have two perspectives on the LCDT. One is suffused with feelings of personal attachment and affection. I was part of something that had impact and significance and this has been of enormous importance to me. The second arises from a place which is more detached from the past and which is related to an affection for dance in general. From that standpoint, if the LCDT left no continuing influence, I would not really mind. As long as there is vital, creative and stimulating dance in Britain which is connected to the people, reflecting back the concerns of the people, and challenging the assumptions of the people, I think that's wonderful. If it is judged that the LCDT had a hand in bringing about that situation, I will find that immensely gratifying.

RM: Was there anything going on in the LCDT that has been lost?

CB: I am sure that there were a number of things which were lost. One specific thing largely disappeared partly as a result of a policy consideration as well as changing realities. This concerned the viability of repertory dance companies at a time when choreographer-led companies began to proliferate. There was a paper produced at the Arts Council which suggested that choreographer-led companies represented the way of the future and that repertory companies were of less relevance. This was written at a time when the fate of the LCDT was hanging in the balance. Interestingly, recently Richochet Dance Company was cited by a national newspaper as being the harbinger of a new future for dance, so perhaps the demise of the repertory dance company was exaggerated! And, of course, companies like Rambert Dance Company continue to thrive.

RM: Can we reminisce for a while. You and I both danced with the LCDT. There is something that is difficult to grasp now: the atmosphere of what was going on in that company. I remember when you first came and watched a rehearsal of the company. I think you said you could not tell when the rehearsal began and when it ended.

CB: Yes I remember that.

RM: Do you think there was something special in its processes, in the early days of the company, that was evident in the rehearsal room?

CB: Yes, clearly it was like no other rehearsal room I had ever been in. My impression was that it was special within Britain at that point. There was an atmosphere, an ethos, something about the way that creativity permeated the interaction.

You can point to other things that were special. For instance, the way in which the production of *Stages* appealed to a young audience, many of them university students. This seems to be one of the first times that the link between dance and young people, particularly students, was made in such a firm and direct way. Students were discovering dance as a means of contemporary expression which meant something to them. It was not the same as taking a ballet to a college audience; the LCDT spoke to them about their own culture. In *Stages*, which was named after the poem by Herman Hesse, students found something relevant to their own lives, so in this event there was something, sociologically interesting and important for dance.

RM: Concerning that "something that was interesting and important", the early Modern Dancers had a sense that they were doing something of deep importance, even of religious importance. Cohan had something of that attitude, well . . . a lot of that. He suggested that his dancers should go through a transformative experience and even that the witnesses in the audience might go through important change. Do you think that attitude was in this country before?

CB: To answer that would involve complete speculation on my part. I assume because the feelings you are speaking about are human feelings and have manifested in other cultures at other times, at some point those feelings must have been manifest here in the UK, perhaps in George Fox or the Methodist preachers. Whether those things occurred in the UK in dance before, I simply could not say.

RM: You were in a ballet company before you entered the LCDT. Between these two jobs you went off on a journey, in India I think. Then you entered the LCDT and stayed for a large part of your career. Might this be because that company offered the opportunity for a journey of significance which was internal rather than geographical.

CB: It's an interesting speculation. I am happier focusing on practical elements, elements of which I have direct experience. I am happier focusing on my engagement with the physical information which was being imparted in the teaching, as well as the creative processes. Something special was imparted in the teaching of what we might call the technique. It was clear that every physical process had a mental or intellectual impulse behind it. I was remaking the physical being with which I engage in this world. We all were doing that. That, for me, was an extremely profound experience. I still draw on that experience. I still, in a very physical sense, draw on the experience of having found a centre and achieving that centre as a kind of home point. It can be a point of rest, of the initiation of movement, of the initiation of energy. Even if I have to speak at a conference I will be looking for that point. I first found this experience at The Place, at the LCDT. That discovery, for me, could be found only in that company at that particular time. There was a direct relationship between the way the so-called technique was taught and a philosophical stance which I found very interesting, in fact compelling.

RM: You are speaking of a centre that is physical, emotional and supra-emotional. This brings us back to Cohan, who most influenced what went on in that company, particularly when we talk about the technique of the first half of the twenty-one years of the LCDT. He was trying to change people through a physical process and change them in a much more than physical way. Do you think that is going on as a conscious project now in this country?

CB: Perhaps the consciousness in dance is changing in other ways now, for instance with the interaction of sports science and dance training. The context now is so very different than in the early days of the LCDT when there was much less dance activity and much less dance information.

If we looked at the dance listings from *Time Out* magazine from the late 60s and early 70s we could get a sense of the scale and nature of dance activity at that point. If we then compared that to the listings available to us today in *Time Out* and other sources such as *Juice*, produced by The Place Dance Services, then we could compare what exists today with what existed then. I am sure we would see that we could participate in dance sessions based on anything from *capoeira* to Humphrey technique. While a cynic might say that this is an example of the commodification of dance, it does represent a huge growth. It reminds us that the world of dance has changed enormously in the past decades.

In a way the LCDT contributed to this by introducing an alternative to the dominance of ballet in the late 60s and early 70s.

RM: So there has been a flood in the provision of dance technique since the late 1960s when the LCDT and Rambert introduced Modern or Contemporary Dance to the UK. Now is there some essential attitude to dance and art, and even the place of art in life, which was championed by the LCDT which isn't pegged to a certain system of a class or to any dance technique? A new attitude towards what dance can do existed among the early Modern Dancers. Cohan seemed of that school. The beginnings of The Royal Ballet and Ballet Rambert, which took place at the same time in the UK as Modern Dance developed in the USA and Europe, did not show this attitude in the same way. Perhaps Antony Tudor did in some of his work, but he went away. What was that unusual and essential thing in American and European Modern Dance and is it still here and if its still here what value is it?

CB: Those are difficult and wide-ranging questions! In focusing on the underlying beliefs, I agree that there is a discernible pattern in the information which comes to us from the early Modern Dancers and this suggests a somewhat shared belief system was present. Of course it could be argued that in any set of aesthetics there is a belief system which is interwoven to some extent. The founders of Modern Dance, Isadora Duncan, Ruth St Denis, Doris Humphrey and Martha Graham were people with large ideas, large thoughts and deep thoughts. I agree that there were a number of ideas which imparted to us in the early days of the LCDT some directly, some subliminally.

RM: Laban did dances about the "swinging temple" and spoke of dance performances as "sacred acts". He founded a "dance farm" which was very like a religious community. Ruth St Denis, besides taking that name, danced as a goddess. So again with early Modern Dancers the religious aspect was right out front. They accepted the notion that they were religious leaders or almost so. Graham both implied such claims and repudiated them. Cohan did not claim to be a quasi-religious leader. He would say, however, that you, as his dancer, had to change in some way that was more than physical.

You mentioned "the centre" which makes me think of *haragei*, as associated with Zen Buddhism, within the Japanese martial arts, in which the finding of a more than physical centre brings a kind of enlightenment. There seems to have existed the idea in early Modern Dancers, and in the LCDT of Cohan when it was strong, that dance could do this. It could provide some kind of enlightenment.

CB: Yes it may be that was the case and it may be that some shared that belief more strongly than others. Some may not have been overtly aware of it. Of course, we were young people. Things were unfolding before us; they were exciting times. There was the feeling we were on an energizing, interesting and demanding journey.

RM: There is influence from the LCDT, for example, on Anthony Van Laast who has been very successful in commercial musical theatre. He has exploited theatricality by dancing within sets with a sophisticated use of lighting which the LCDT was known for in its day. Then there was influence on rebels like Robert North who set out, even while in the LCDT, to do non-serious dances, within the serious-minded LCDT, which were successful and very funny and even populist. There were many such cases and I am trying to determine if there is something essential in them which is not only statistics. There was an enormous energy and influence. This could just be put down to the size of the company and the amount of money put into it and, as you said earlier, that it was the only such large Contemporary company then except for Rambert. Did it influence things because it made a big noise and produced a lot of people? But we could say that about any big company like, say, The Royal Ballet. Is there any influence which is not the result simply of size and consequent general spin off that we could identify?

CB: Again it may be too soon to say, although as things move on these assessments also become more difficult. To assess the influence of the LCDT in this way would be a complex endeavour. There was a certain attitude which pervaded the work and Robert Cohan and Robin Howard had immense influence, not just over the LCDT, but also over a school and a theatre. I don't know to what extent it is common knowledge, but Robin also had a great interest in the mind/body movement and in alternative therapies and in alternative views of the world. No doubt these factors influenced the work of the LCDT.

RM: A lot of young dancers working now have heard of the LCDT but know nothing else of it. There are a number of people teaching the core technique taught by Cohan but there is a great deal else around. Do young dancers, say in their mid-twenties, derive any influence from this company?

CB: We have used the word "influence" in relation to a number of things connected with the LCDT but this question gives me the opportunity to clarify some thoughts. In fact this question reminds me of a confusion which arose for me in a conversation with Bob Cohan in the early 80s. The conversation was in a theatre during a dress rehearsal; Bob made a reference to the possibility that "the work" would disappear from Britain. I was not sure what he meant and so I asked him; I interpreted his reply to mean that he feared that work based on Graham technique would disappear. I was amazed as I had never understood that the preservation of the Graham-based technique had anything to do with the work of the LCDT. What I thought we were doing was unfolding a kind of creative journey in the UK which would flow through a number of pathways and in myriad forms. I did not feel that I was attached to a specific fixed artistic credo and perhaps that was naïve of me.

I may not be being absolutely, intellectually rigorous in saying that, since there was clearly an artistic direction to the company, but I had not considered that the future was constrained by the technique used for training. I assumed that the repertoire would change and grow and so that the training would need to change and grow.

When we talk of transformative dance, I think that that experience is intrinsic to a lot of dance and that's one reason why people dance, have danced and continue to dance. I think this can be true in clubs and discos and that some people are finding a connection to ritual and a sense of change and transformation through that ritual.

In the case of Cohan's work with the LCDT, I feel that it is possible to separate certain principles which were being transmitted from the vehicle of transmission, the vehicle in this instance being the Graham-based technique. Some of the principles were related to a deep analysis of movement and the flowing of energies within the body. Both of these were predicated on a consciousness which needed to be honed with rigour and a belief that one could change. This last may be the key point as it almost requires a moment of faith – the faith that one can change and direct that change through the application of intelligence. This implies a sense of responsibility about one's state in which awareness and motivation are coupled with intelligent action in order to enable change.

As far as the actual physical technique is concerned, there is at least a video of Cohan's class. I mention it partly because so much dance information concerning training has been lost to us and although the video was not produced in ideal conditions, it does exist and so we have access to some of his teaching.

RM: We might continue to investigate dance as a transformative practice. Cohan's work, particularly in the early years, could be compared to that of Grotowski, who began to be known a little earlier. The studio was a place where people were transformed. One of Cohan's titles is *Place Of Change*. Grotowski used the term "Art as Vehicle". In your period in the LCDT was dance a vehicle in Grotowski's sense of a vehicle to something else?

CB: For me it was a transformative experience and so dance was a vehicle. I had the sense that this was true for others and for Bob Cohan himself. I also think that he intended at least some of his work to be that; however, at some point this aspect was obscured or even lost.

RM: It slipped away within the working time of the company?

CB: Yes.

RM: The change we are talking about, is it of any value? Of course we are changing all the time in ways that may not be important.

CB: If we are going to judge if the change is of value then we can ask the person who was changed. So I can ask was the experience valuable to me? Yes it was enormously valuable to me and I am delighted that I was there at that time. Was that experience of value to others in Britain? Again I would have to say yes and this was evident in an enormous flowering of dance activity. There may have been some negative attributes also. It would be astonishing if there were not.

RM: Grotowski used the word "translumination". In a conversation with Peter Brook, the latter says he works on the basis of the relationship between the actor, the director and the audience. Grotowski replies that this is valid but for him too complicated. He works on the potential of the relationship between the actor and the director. This relationship can lead to transformative experience that he calls "translumination" which is a kind of enlightenment for both. Enlightenment is a kind of being filled with light. This is getting close to William James' "noetic" experience or experience which gives knowledge and is one of the two "marks" which, he says, characterize all mystical experience. So there is transformative experience which leaves behind knowledge. It is very likely Cohan was working through an attitude informed by such thought. I am not sure to what extent he understood that he was. Quite possibly he did. Grotowski's work had already been published.

CB: Cohan once told me that he had an early interest in the work of Gurdjieff and was involved in this to some extent in New York before he came to the UK.

RM: So did the company have a transluminative effect on its members?

CB: For me it did at times, but I am making this judgement in relation to my understanding of these things which might be limited. Of course we are reflecting on things which took place some time ago and so our evaluations might be coloured by our feelings for the past. It is also difficult to recall any particular point at which we discussed these aspects of the work while we were actively engaged in it.

I think that a number of members of the company had some idea about the work and that those ideas affected the way in which they worked. Others may have worked very well but were engaged at a different level. I don't think that one experience is more valid than another. I don't even know if an awareness of other levels of engagement made me a better dancer; sometimes I think it interfered in my ability to dance. Some of the influences of the LCDT on my life have been mundane and others have been subtle and powerful.

Returning to the theatre, in which I include dance, I agree with Brook that the witness is key. Since relationship of the witness to the performance is a key it is important to find out if a transformative experience was provided for witnesses. From my limited experience, I would say that it was for some people. At some point when that aspect disappeared for them, those people felt bitterly disappointed.

RM: In its latter days the LCDT no longer gave the kind of transformative experience it once had. Whatever influence there was, at one point it was of a certain quality and later it wasn't. It's like a dancer who dances too long; the decadence can be what is remembered.

CB: In my view a lot of this is directly related to the creativity of Robert Cohan and the way in which his sense of excitement and discovery developed and changed. When other choreographers, for example Sue [Siobhan Davies] and Robert [North] began contribution to the repertoire, they were also caught up in this adventure. But later Robert Cohan, through no fault of his own, became exhausted from working full out for so long. He was doing too many things and a lot of them were connected to the Contemporary Dance Trust. Much of his creative energy was taken from him. Of course it is important to remember that the LCDT had a number of other important contributors, among them directors such as Nancy Duncan and Dan Wagoner. The area you seem to be investigating, however, appears to be connected to the contribution of Robert Cohan and, therefore, inextricably connected to his creative energy.

RM: Concerning the way you teach here now, or provide an environment where others teach, can you say if there is any influence from the LCDT?

CB: Of course there has been an influence, but I do not promote it in a conscious way. The LCDT represents an important phase in the dance history of the UK and so I feel students should be aware of it just as they should be aware of other aspects. However, there are undoubtedly influences from my past experiences of which I am not aware. In any case I have a general sense of gratitude to all of my past teachers, especially Robert Cohan, for their teaching. I received the teaching and whether I am aware of its influence, I accept it as part of my history in dance.

RM: As we are affected by all sorts of things whether we wish to be or not, is there anything within the fourteen years you were at the LCDT that you wish had never touched you?

CB: That's close to asking if I have any regrets. Of course there are quite a few things which one wishes had not happened. But those things are all part of the unfolding of experience and what one regrets may be the very things that allows a deeper reflection. Without those challenges one would not reflect so deeply. I wish that I had had a greater range of experiences in dance, but a dance career is fleeting. I attempt to accept it all and hope that I do so in good grace.

Figure 7
Siobhan Davies, Namron in *The Calm*. Choreography, Siobhan Davies.
Photo: Anthony Crickmay. Courtesy of V&A Picture Library.

# Foundational Technique, Choreography and Creative Discipline: An Interview with Christopher Bruce

Ross McKim

At: The Rambert Dance Company Studios, Chiswick
On: 30 June 1998

CB: It is certainly true that the LCDT had a dramatic effect, and still has an effect, on the present dance scene. I think what is happening today could not have happened without the LCDT. It certainly influenced me in a variety of ways. Maybe I should go back to Rambert and to the days when there were these two middle-scale Contemporary companies existing side by side, each with its own distinctive style. Rambert was more Classically based, even though we did Graham training as well as Ballet. I would say we were more traditional in our outlook, whereas London Contemporary was very much founded on Contemporary Dance technique. Rambert made work from wider, more eclectic sources which were both Classical and Contemporary. London Contemporary was more tightly formed around Contemporary technique, basically Graham, which evolved and developed with the repertoire and growth of the in-house choreographers. Bob (Robert Cohan), Sue (Siobhan Davies) and Robert (North), amongst others. They quickly developed a strong and innovative repertoire formed around their technical base.

I don't know whether the Ballet Rambert of that time particularly influenced London Contemporary but I do know London Contemporary influenced me. I'll tell you about something that happened within Rambert in the '70s. I had discussions with Norman (Morrice) and others, constructive arguments I think, in which I was critical of some areas of our work. We were strong in tremendous personalities and we all moved with energy and passion. I felt, however, that some of the work we were performing was compositionally rather amorphous and the dancing, a little undisciplined on occasions (including my own dancing I might add). If we could balance the emotional impact the company had with tighter technical control, we would be the better for it. Others disagreed with me and I think that Norman was afraid we might lose some of the passionate commitment many people enjoyed at Rambert performances. In 1974, I became Associate Director of the company under John Chesworth's direction and I began to push for some of my ideas. I don't think I was always popular for it and some perceived me as being ruthless. I was still only twenty-nine years of age, really too young for the position, but I do think that there was a strong development at Rambert from the mid-70s. The Company was arguably at its best from this period on, under its various directors. I'm not suggesting that I was entirely responsible for this; there were many talented individuals who made up what I feel was a very unique and powerful group of artists. Many of the principles I fought for over that period, having observed other companies I admired, including LCDT, are the same as I have applied to the present day company.

RM: The LCDT went through some unsuccessful times during the period when it and Rambert were running simultaneously as companies of about the same size. At one point it did certain work which some people liked very much but which generally emptied the house. I wondered if seeing these problems taking place influenced attitudes here at Rambert?

CB: Yes, because unless a situation exists where one has unlimited funding to play with and little pressure to bring in audiences, the box office has to be an important consideration. Often, there's the problem that work of quality does not attract a large audience. RDC needs the box office income to make ends meet and we are committed to developing our audiences. We are trying to maintain quality and innovation alongside accessibility. It's a balancing act, very difficult to maintain. I just hope that things here never get as bad as the present situation in the US where, due to lack of support from government, no one can really take the risks that are essential for the development of new work. It's tragic considering that the US is really the home of so many of the Modern Dance movements that influence the artform today. The LCDT went through its stronger periods as well as its troughs, as did Rambert. It was interesting to see the two companies evolving and going through their various crises. I think it was very good for each company to have the other one around. There was a wonderful balance and a healthy rivalry which helped keep us on our toes (metaphorically speaking). It's more than sad that we have lost a major repertory company for Contemporary Dance.

RM: You say you felt the choreography of your company, for a time, was not tight.

CB : That's right. I was observing not only LCDT which was strongly based on Graham, but also the ballet-based Netherlands Dance Theatre. I was looking mainly at these two important forces in dance at that time. They were strictly disciplined, technically speaking, in their totally different ways. Rambert was always an emotionally exciting company to watch but I think we had the ability to balance this with technical and choreographic strength more fully in the '70s into the '80s. There were always strong works in the repertoire; however I sometimes felt that before that time we were still finding our feet. We were basing our work on so many styles which we were not controlling, so that our identity was not always clear. That is why, coming back to Rambert now, I have been very strict about class discipline and although the rep is very varied, I have tried to limit the variety of styles we are dealing with at any one time. On occasions in the past, Rambert perhaps leaned heavily towards an emotional theatricality. It is an area I enjoy and is encompassed within my present policy, but there has to be a balance if you want to cover a range of work successfully.

RM: Particularly in the 1970s, Cohan taught the LCDT company class most days and dominated its teaching in general. A director/choreo-grapher was working also at a teaching level in a company or at a technical process level before or prior to rehearsal. Did that limit the LCDT or make them unusual?

CB: Both. I think that having Bob there, working in that way was a tremendous asset. Things went wrong when this base became dis-sipated, partly because Bob withdrew as he got older, (which is understandable) and this basic core discipline wasn't replaced. Many different technical and choreographic influences began to feed into the company, but it seemed that nothing was holding all these elements together. It was beginning to come together again with Dan Wagoner, particularly towards the end of his time there. That was my impression and I thought it sad that his time with the Company could not have continued for longer. When I went there to make work, I found the Company rather demoralized. They had been through a hell of a time and, despite the quality of the dancers and Cohan holding things together on a temporary basis, they were beginning to fragment under the stress and insecurity of an unknown future. Understandably, this was not helping general discipline. I very much enjoyed working with them but I was concerned that a lack of strong leadership and direction was doing great harm. Having said that, when the end was in sight, the dancers were magnificent in the way they pulled together and fought for their survival. Of course, they did survive in another form under Richard Alston. So, all was not lost.

On the question of discipline generally; times have changed. With that change I feel it is sometimes harder to hold on to the necessary level of discipline required for a company to function at its best. I see this problem increasing, particularly with some of the larger companies. Freedom requires so much self-discipline, which makes it tougher for the dancers. We all need someone to support and drive us. And we need to continue taking criticism on board, continue developing the level of our work. I had people like Marie Rambert and Norman Morrice supporting me in this way and I feel extremely fortunate that I had that help. Without a driving force it is impossible, even with a company of the quality and heritage of the LCDT, to hold things together for long. What is difficult for me to understand is that with all the wonderful people that evolved from that company (it created an astounding variety of special artists: yourself, Anthony [Van Laast], Sue [Davies], Patrick [Harding-Irmer], Robert [North] and Darshan [Singh Bhuller] – I am leaving out many names) when the crisis came there was no one to take the reins. I found it astonishing that the future was not somehow better prepared for. But, I guess one can't prepare for every eventuality. I think that losing Dan was very unfortunate. Then, of course, it just didn't work out with his successor.

RM: Cohan was strong on the basis of the Graham work. In the early '70s he seemed to believe that, in dance, there were things that were right and things that were wrong. He seemed to believe that Graham was right and aspects of ballet were wrong, at least for his company. This gave him a focus. I wonder if any of his possible successors had any of the same level of conviction they could lean on.

CB: They couldn't have done it in the same way as Bob. You are into new territory now. It's a different world for Contemporary Dance. Whoever might have taken over couldn't have done it from a Graham base. Not anymore. What should replace it, given the developments within the Contemporary Dance scene? You have to make a choice. At Rambert our Modern teaching is usually based on Cunningham. Richard Alston is similarly based. I believe it to be a very solid and comprehensive form of training if it is well taught. The real problem today is that there is such a range of physical demands on a dancer that no single technique properly prepares you for them all. In taking this job (director of Rambert Dance Company) I have chosen to use Classical Ballet technique as a base. Marie Rambert believed very firmly that if you were a well-trained and disciplined Classical dancer, you had the foundation to do anything. To a certain extent this is true, but to do "anything" you still require the appropriate training. While there are many Classical dancers who will never make Contemporary dancers, Classical Ballet gives us a strong base. Look at the variety of work Rambert is now able to perform. The work of Tudor (on point), Cunningham, mine, Sue Davies, Kylian, Bob Cohan, Jeremy James,

Per Jonsson and many others; such a variety of styles. The dancers have managed to cope because they are of an extremely high standard and because apart from the Ballet training, they take regular Contemporary classes. It is hard on their bodies but I know of no other way of maintaining a real ability to cope with integrity with such a variety of work. I believe we are the only major company in the world at present which maintains this policy consistently. I should add that, when we are able, we try to tailor the Modern training appropriately. For example when Bob Cohan was mounting *Stabat Mater* we trained in Graham for a time.

RM: Was it time for the LCDT to end when it did given that Graham technique was its basis?

CB: The Graham basis had been largely left behind by the time the LCDT closed. No, I don't think it was time for a repertory-based LCDT to end. Mind you, it would have taken a clear and strong artistic vision and a lot more money to make it work, but I think Bob's ideas were sound. The problem would have been finding the right group of people to lead it. The company should have continued but it would have had to be a different kind of company, much in the way that the Rambert Company became different when Marie Rambert gave up the direction. That happened again when Norman (Morrice) left, when it was under John (Chesworth), when it was under Robert (North) and then Richard (Alston) and now, me. Each, a different face for the Company. There is a line, but the accent is changed. It sheds a skin regularly and is reborn. That is what needed to happen at the LCDT. You had to carry something through but someone had to take it into the next phase. The more I think about it, though, I believe this has happened with Richard creating a company out of the remnants of the LCDT. The change has been greater in that it is now a one choreographer-led company, the name has changed and, for the moment, there are fewer performances. But there is still a link with Bob and Robin Howard's creation. So, maybe we should not be in mourning. One thing is for sure. You cannot keep a company alive solely for historic reasons; it must also have an artistically valid reason for existing.

RM: You have your Rambert tradition here which is based on the almost mythological character of Marie Rambert. At the LCDT although the tradition came from Graham, the source of inspiration and energy was very largely Cohan. When he went . . . .

CB: I saw the company a couple of times under Dan (Wagoner) and I liked what he was doing. He did some very successful work. You could see him working in a particular direction. There was a purpose.

RM: Rambert Dance Company has survived and is healthy. The last few times I went to the LCDT I was not sure it could continue. Whatever had been so wonderful five to ten years ago. . . .

CB: The London Contemporary Company, in the few years before it went, was certainly in trouble. But things also got pretty difficult at Rambert from time to time. If you've created an institution, and built up all that history you don't just throw it away. See, what can be rebuilt from what remains. I think it was a question of finding people who could take the LCDT on to another level, in a different direction. That didn't seem to happen from within at the time. Richard, however, who was very much part of the company's history, has rebuilt a company from what existed.

RM: Some of Robin Howard's prophecies fulfilled themselves. He said that the LCDT would have accomplished what it set out to do when all the people it brought up disagreed with it and went off to do their own things. That is what he got. The protection of a large subsidized group was lost. Even Richard is a project company as is Sue (Siobhan Davies).

Can we talk of you as a dancer? Norman Morrice seemed to use Glen Tetley to open up eyes to the Graham possibility. This included your young eyes.

CB: It was the classes of Anna Price and Clover Roope that were crucial to the work of the company. Both of them were marvellous dancers themselves and excellent teachers. Then, when Glen came along, we were suddenly introduced to a Modern dancer and choreographer who had worked for and alongside many of the great artists of American Contemporary Dance in the early to middle part of the century. As with many dancers in the US, at that time, he crossed the lines between Contemporary Dance, Ballet, Musical Theatre and Film. This is still the only way many dancers can survive economically in the States. His movement vocabulary was so rich. We were already fusing styles at Rambert but he brought an integrity and a germ of where everything came from. It was wonderful to watch him move and we learned so much from working with him. His Ballets were certainly the pillars of our repertory for a considerable time. The only problem was that his influence was very, very strong. I and other choreographer/dancers from within the company tended to take a while before we could develop a voice that was individual and not dominated by a "Tetley" look. In my opinion, this was especially dangerous because the plasticity of the movement and fusion of styles could degenerate into something very woolly. Even his own Ballets suffered if they were not well rehearsed or had dancers performing them who did not have the required Con-temporary technique. The movement could very easily look lightweight and peripheral. With Glen's work you had to see that the movement came from the centre and, how ever classical the dance appeared, it still employed the Graham principal of contraction and release. Mixing genres is quite dangerous and it requires strong technical discipline. This brings us back to what we were discussing at the beginning of the interview. The freedom and variety of Rambert's multi-discipline approach made for a wealth of opportunities creatively but was difficult to control. It led to the loose or amorphous quality I became critical of. And that is why Cohan's approach, though eventually possibly a limitation to LCDT's development, gave his company a strength and cohesion. Overall, the Ballet Rambert of that period had some wonderful Ballets that ranged through the choreography of Tudor, Sokolow, Morrice, Tetley and many others including emerging choreographers within the Company such as myself, Chesworth, Jonathan Taylor among others. So, one must not over-stress the negative. It's important, however, to be critical if there is to be any development.

RM: Clover Roope and maybe Anna Price were among those people Robin Howard had sent to study with Graham in New York so that is an influence on Rambert from the Contemporary Dance Trust. I'm pushing the point concerning Glen Tetley because he perhaps allowed you at Rambert to appreciate more deeply this influence which was otherwise being supplied by the LCDT.

CB: He was the first influence that made us understand American Modern Dance more fully and demonstrate how it could be used in a freer form. We were already doing this by melding, sometimes successfully, sometimes not, Graham and classical technique. It took a while to evolve individual languages for our dances. Norman Morrice had already begun the process before 1966 after he had spent time studying in New York. This is often forgotten. He created the new Rambert of '66 which led to everything that followed. I have already mentioned Anna Sokolow. From the mid-70s, Louis Falco, though he only made one piece for us, had a terrific influence through his Limon technique-based work and the way he fused it with his remarkable qualities as a dancer.

RM: Something came together in your own body. You were a very special dancer. You were able to learn to move in a certain new way. And you started choreographing while you were dancing a lot.

CB: Learning the first two works Glenn mounted for us *Pierrot Lunaire* and *Ricercare,* was a terribly difficult experience. One learned a tremendous amount, not just about coping with the technical challenges but also welding them together to create an expressive vocabulary. I would say that, after the Graham classes, Tetley was the biggest influence on my dance career and my work as a choreographer. In fact, it took me some time to escape from it and evolve my own language.

RM: Cohan once said he was not sure he was a choreographer. It seems that for him, like some others who worked with Graham, the excitement of that period of their lives caused everything else, including their own work, to be a let down. One can have an influence that is too powerful.

CB: I think that's true.

RM: As concerns choreographic influences on you from the LCDT; Richard came here, Robert came here, Sue is working with you now. Have you been influenced by them?

CB: I was influenced by every choreographer that has come here: Manuel Alum, Luis Falco and the others. I was used in all their work and I was like a sponge soaking it up. My job then was to absorb and digest the experience in a way that could enrich my own vocabulary. I also had the influence of all my training, from the age of eleven, in Tap Dancing as well as Ballet. Later, the Graham and Cunningham techniques plus all the choreographers I ever worked with, even the character classes I studied at The Rambert School were of value. Also, my work with actors and singers. I'm a choreographer who enjoys all aspects of the arts. I have absorbed all these disciplines. If you could see what I am doing in the studio at present, you would observe all these influences in one way or another. There is always the Classical line but you also see the use of the back and torso and my need always to convey an idea or emotion in performance. The challenge is to mould all these disciplines into a language which is personally mine. I have to be influenced in a way that does not make me like anyone else.

RM: The tradition Cohan came out of was life changing. Dance was something very serious; among the early Modern Dancers it was down-right religious. Cohan would speak almost mystically to his young company when I was in it. Has any of this tradition rubbed off on you?

CB: Despite the great importance to me of my family life, dance has been an overwhelming force in my life. It takes your body and soul and it doesn't let go, at least not in my case. There are times when I thought I'd had enough; certainly my body has felt like it. But somehow it drags you back. Returning to Rambert, it just felt right, like completing the circle. I joinied Rambert School at thirteen and it's been an almost pre-destined and very logical line throughout my life. It could have been broken at any point but it seems I'm attached to dance and Rambert. The cord will not easily sever; however, when the time comes for me to move on, I would like to feel that I will be able to do so without too much of a problem.

RM: That is not out of influence from the LCDT but it may put you in the same serious tradition. It makes you a person working out of an attitude similar to that of Cohan.

CB: Maybe. Though I am very influenced by the lady up there [a photograph of Marie Rambert on the wall] and that whole generation of Bob's, I like to think I'm a freer spirit. I have always had my family life as a balance. That's what has helped to keep me sane. It's enabled me to stay in there. I see myself as a bridge between several generations of dance makers and their different kinds of approach. I have tried to understand the younger generation and stay in touch with them but I do sometimes feel my age.

RM: You are a very successful choreographer who has dealt with particularly serious themes in a consistent way. One could argue that important choreographers like Frederick Ashton, for example, did not do that. Just as you are tied to dance, you have tied it to a serious vein of thought.

CB: I've always lived in the real world while many dancers live only in the art form itself. They live in a sheltered world and don't allow the outside world to touch it. I have always been influenced by life in general. I read a great deal; my main subject has been history which ties up with world events of the present. You see patterns in these events and what is happening politically. Also, I come from a working class background; both my parents appreciated the arts but my life involved me with certain day-to-day realities. My father was fiercely left wing and carried the scars of the 1930s Depression. His attitudes certainly affected me. All this has helped to keep my feet on the ground. So, I am tied to this dance world but I've always had one foot outside it. I have sometimes actually felt I do not quite belong in this world of theatre. There are sides of it I cannot bear, but I love what the theatre can create. I would like to feel that my work has truly had an affect on that world outside. I know this has happened in small ways; the letters from individuals, the use Amnesty International has made of the *Swansong* video, what *Ghost Dances* meant to so many Chileans who saw it as it was passed around in secret. Yes, I try to keep that one foot outside, firmly on the ground.

RM: Could you say, what remains from the LCDT?

CB: You have to look at the people working in the business today that came through the system. You, working in Rambert School, will bring all you learnt in the LCDT into your work there. Siobhan Davies is a major choreographic influence now. She has probably turned out to be the most important choreographer to emerge from the school and company. Robert North has had a big influence and is making work around the world. Richard Alston did not dance with the Company but he choreographed for it. Darshan is choreographing. I am naming only a few of the talented people who emerged through LCDT. There are many former LCDT dancers teaching around the world. Anthony Van Laast has had a tremendously successful career in the commercial theatre. These tentacles would not have appeared and grown had it not been for the LCDT. That's a terrific achievement. The LCDT School is a major organization and force within the dance world as is The Place Theatre. There are many smaller companies that emerged out of LCDT. All this is the legacy of Cohan and Howard's pioneering work over three decades.

# A Contemporary Dance "Family" and Infrastructure: An Interview with Richard Alston

Ross McKim

At: The Place
On: 25 August 1998

RM: Do you feel influence remains from the London Contemporary Dance Theatre on the Contemporary Dance scene of today?

RA: The Contemporary Dance Trust created a whole infrastructure for contemporary dance in this country. Its performance company, in particular, filled a certain niche in the circuit of theatres, for theatre managers, for programmers. Now that it is not there, people don't quite know how to replace it. For a long time LCDT was complementary to Rambert. People accused them of being too similar but I think they had very different functions. This is particularly seen to be so because Rambert once again has a fairly strong classical emphasis and there is no real equivalent in the Contemporary field.

Here at The Place, there are now fewer young people drawn to the school through seeing a contemporary dance company in their local theatre. Attracting students to its school was always part of the huge influence LCDT had all over the country. Young people could see dancers such as yourself and Robert North and later on Jonathan Lunn, Darshan (Singh Bhuller) and Lauren Potter. That was so inspiring for young people on a very basic level and gave them a vision of where training might lead.

RM: Maybe we could consider the LCDT's history in periods. There was the very early period when it gave occasional concerts and was a mixture of students of its school and stars brought from New York. Then there was a period when it worked in this theatre here, about 250 seats.[1] Then the company toured middle-scale theatres. Finally it began to tour large-scale theatres. You were here from the beginning. Do you

33

**Figure 8**
**Richard Alston rehearsing. Photo: Liam Daniel. Courtesy of V&A Picture Library.**

think there was anything in the influence of this organization that wouldn't have found its way into the UK anyway. There was American influence coming into British dance through Rambert and in other ways?

RA: I think there was a big difference between Rambert and the LCDT even in the beginning, perhaps especially so then. Although Rambert had very visionary ideas, there was a tremendous feeling of protectiveness for this established name: "Ballet Rambert." As students, of LSCD, we were terribly purist about Rambert performances. We'd think, "it's ballet . . . there are arabesques." If you talked to dancers at Rambert at the time you'd find their skirmishes with Graham work were sort of motley. They would very often do a full classical barre before they began any Graham floor work. Later, when I was there, Rambert became more of a Modern Dance company, by default really because that is my background. So at that time it became more like London Contemporary. Yet London Contemporary still retained a different role. There was a kind of weightiness and physicality that was much gutsier, much less pretty than Rambert. Though the Rambert men had a rather macho image, the women were always very slender and lightweight. In the early days the LCDT exercised an enormous influence by choosing dancers with a different kind of body and with a different sort of mindset. The irony is that Bob, being such a knowledgeable and detailed teacher, became more and more involved with physical perfection and ended up making dancers who were sleek and long limbed.

RM: We don't now have a big Contemporary Dance company working as Bob and you do, where the director is involved at a pre-choreography and pre-rehearsal level. Cohan taught company class every day or had people do so who taught in his vein. And he looked, quite consciously, for things which were an alternative to Ballet. You fall in those footsteps. You have always taught a lot and enjoyed teaching.

RA: My recent work has more of a connection with my roots as an artist, as a dancer. I spent a dozen years at Rambert. When I was there certain things were a given, such as being able to work with a quite large ensemble of dancers. They were good dancers, but the majority of them were fundamentally classically trained and not much experienced in contemporary work. Some years later we had a meeting with the dancers at Rambert to discuss injury. The dancers said, "we think that with the kind of work we are doing we ought to have three Modern classes and two Classical classes a week and not three Classical and two Modern classes a week." That sounds banal and numerical but actually it was a huge change. The dancers knew there was material in the Contemporary class which was going to protect their backs. They were using their backs so much working for me and Sue Davies. When I was at Rambert, I was willing to be influenced by different kinds of training, seeing how that could feed my work. Now I really am enjoying being directly back in touch with my own physicality with all its restrictions and weaknesses. The movement that I make now is much more weighty and juicy.

Being back in this building has reminded me about how that weightiness felt. These are the rooms in which I used to take class; Bob Cohan used to laugh at me as I fell over. This is where I danced and trained and this is where all that energy and vigour was, where I had my formative physical sensations.

It's how I was trained and it's how I used to move. These days, I'm back in the studio more than I used to be and I teach all the time. My work has evolved into something quite different from the Cunningham work that I studied when I went to New York. The movement I make now is much less lifted and tense and not so linear. It's more fluid and weighty . . . I keep saying that word but there it is.

RM: In my time here we associated you with bringing the Cunningham influence to the UK. I suppose you did not do it alone but you were very much associated with it in this building where Graham was often considered, not only good, but the only good.

RA: Part of that was rebellion. Part of that was a young person looking at

Robin and Bob and thinking, "well, someone should question them." Robin understood that and Bob does now, though I think it irritated him at the time. When I first came here I was completely in awe of Bob and Noemi Lapzezon and Bob Powell and all those wonderful dancers from the Graham Company. But there was the simple fact that my physique, like that of a lot of men, made Graham hard work to put it mildly . . . sitting on the floor in a wide open second. My hips were very tight on the floor. So when Viola (Farber) came and we started class standing it was a huge relief. I was amazed to find a physical language in which you could work without pain. Graham technique was always something that I felt useless trying to do.

I'm not criticizing the Graham work. In fact, funnily enough, as I get older I find once again the strength and the articulation of the back in good Graham work is fantastic. Its wonderful to see. There are still parts of my vocabulary very much influenced by the bold sensations in Graham work.

RM: Talking about technique, the influence which Bob was giving came through the Graham technique because that is what he learned. But it could be transmitted in other ways. He had his own ideas and interests and communicated them through that system. There were other things to learn from here at that time like Tai-Chi. You used to do Tai-Chi.

RA: Last year we reconstructed a section from *Combines*, a piece I made in 1972. There are phrases in that dance that are very Tai-Chi influenced. It's quite overt. It's actually amusing to see how undigested it is. It's just there . . . the turn on the heel, the sinking into the earth and the flow of energy. Then later on when I did release work with Mary Fulkerson down at Dartington, this same flow of energy through the body was one of the basic principles.

One of the reasons I needed a different kind of vocabulary was that I was intuitively drawn towards flowing movement. The Graham work, certainly when Bob first started teaching, was immensely strengthening, but did not evolve into long phrases. Very often there was just one movement and then another. For example, a jump and a contraction, and another jump and contraction. One of the things I responded to in Merce's work and in Classical dance was the small steps which make links within complicated phrases. This led to the whole obsession I still have with working with music. I found that in straight Graham – there are now all sorts of evolved variations of Graham – but in straight Graham the attack was constant and the phrasing quite simple. Mostly her work was dramatically inspired rather than musically motivated.

RM: When one asks what the influence of the choreographic work of the LCDT was, the answer turns out to be complex because it was a repertory company from the beginning. What influence was there on you, if any from Cohan and other people who worked here? Working in the same house when you were a developing young choreographer were Sue, Anna Sokolow, Remy Charlip.

RA: I was young then and I guess I was trying to find my own voice. As you say, this was a house with its own style and I was keen to react against it. The whole choreographic influence here was very much about imagery and rather loaded subjects. This just made me want to run into a clear space and dance about nothing. That's what I was doing even through to *Rainbow Bandit* when I came back from America.

In *Rainbow Bandit* I was also trying to get dancers to move in a different way. Bob was an extraordinary teacher but very analytical. It seemed to me that as the company grew the movement became more and more muscular. I consciously tried to teach a very different kind of fluidity, which dancers like Tom Jobe and Sue (Siobhan Davies) took to like a duck to water. That's how one evolves.

I always thought the dancers here were terrific. The way that the building and the school was set up attracted very talented people. In economically kinder times, it was easier to nurture students through scholarships and through relatively small amounts of money, which Robin provided. So for a long time, fifteen years or so, there was an enormously organic feeling to this building. Don't you think so? Do you remember that? It was a family. When Bob was here there was a company which stayed together. Some people stayed here for fourteen years and more. There was tremendous consistency and a very clear sense of purpose in this building. The mystery for me is how that was not built upon to evolve and develop. That's what I don't understand.

RM: Now you have here a company both like and unlike the LCDT. You do not have some twenty-five dancers and a huge subsidy, but you have a fairly regular group of people. You teach them regularly in some ways as Cohan did; you work at a pre-rehearsal process level. Its interesting to hear you say that you are going back to some of your pre-New York roots. You do seem to be concerned with a depth of physicality though not necessarily in a Graham way. I am not sure you did not do that before you went back to the influence of your early training.

RA: I think I am doing it more strongly now. You can't always keep a clear eye on your own work, but that's how it feels. When I look at the work I did at Rambert, it quite often feels like I was commenting on an existing movement language. For example, I'd think how would it work if I made something different for, say a man who could turn really easily, who could do multiple pirouettes. Now I look back on the work I did at Rambert and suddenly see these pirouettes sitting in the middle and I think "how odd to see them in a piece of mine."

I have always found the connection between process, between class and choreography an enrichment. That is something that I saw for the first time with Bob. There was a company with a very clear sense of unity; everyone knew that they were going to work together in class towards something creative. Later I saw it elsewhere, particularly in the Cunningham studio. I find such a thing exhilarating. It's a vital and important part of the way I myself make work. In that way I was indeed influenced by the family I saw around me at The Place.

RM: There were the ideas that Robin had. He chose Robert Cohan perhaps because he thought Bob was the man to further them. Do you think many of the idealistic plans Robin had for this building and the LCDT got through to you?

RA: I remember Robin with subjective fondness. Now I think that I understand a lot of the things he believed in and I see them going on here at The Place. That is very inspiring. When I was younger, I felt that he had two strong sides to his character. One was visionary and quite wild and believed in something very broad for humanity. Robin felt that dancing could help people get in touch with themselves and achieve a healthy balance between mind and body. The other side of him was totally involved with building his organization. I used to nudge him a bit for taking such a terribly fast route. He said to me with startling honesty: "I can't wait around, Richard, because of my health; I never know if I am going to be alive next month. I need to set something up before I go and it has to be something that the dance establishment will accept." With that side of his mind he was extremely grateful to Bob for being such a strategic and political Artistic Director. I think that side of things became very rapidly established. Things narrowed down and the Company became less and less lively. Then, at the end of his life, Robin knew the company was no longer very healthy. He would always quite purposely startle people by throwing out ideas which would cause us all to think again. At one point he suggested to his fellow board members that the LCDT be closed and that they look for some kind of different model to come out of the school. In the last part of his life he was still absolutely committed to the school.

RM: There is indeed some paradox there. Robin was almost, like De Valois, setting out to build a great national institution. He almost did it and rather quickly in the first ten years. Yet his essential ideas were about transforming individuals through dance. That is an alternative concept. He had those sorts of ideas. Graham, with her Jungian base which she had through people like Joseph Campbell, was concerned with personal transformation. Cohan knew of these things and possessed another set of ideas about transformation, through Gurdjieff.

RA: What you're saying is very important because the Gurdjieff thing disappeared. Everything became very strategic. The audience building, and the numbers and the popularizing became more and more important. It became the forefront of the LCDT policy. At the time the first season was being prepared for East Grinstead (1967), every dancer was told by Bob that he or she should have a Larousse mythology book. This came straight from the Graham company. Everyone there was wandering around with these large picture books. They were all supposed to know their myths. There is something rather nice about that! Later on, the training remained meticulous but the actual product became more and more about reaching a wide audience and less about reaching into oneself.

RM: One thing which is difficult in considering the influence of the LCDT is that it was at least two animals. There is a cut-off point sometime in the late '70s or in the '80s after which it is sometimes depressing to review the progress of the company. Some people only remember its decadence. This went on for the last five or even ten years.

RA: It was the victim of its own time because there was the so-called "dance boom", which, like all booms, came and went. With the Arts Council's approval, the company was building towards quite large theatres where the pressure becomes enormous to put bums on seats. That's when you don't necessarily need your mythology book!

An artistic organization has got to have an identity. It's got to have a centre in order to battle with whatever the difficulties are. If you shift from that centre you are in trouble. I always thought it was a very significant moment in the gradual demise of LCDT when they chose to do *Rooster*. This work came from a Ballet company in Geneva and was choreographed by someone, who no one should have been surprised to find not so long afterwards, becoming the artistic director of Rambert. *Rooster* was immensely successful and the LCDT danced it superbly. But I think it confused people hugely. What was this company becoming?

RM: I remember when the company was still performing in this little theatre here at The Place with its 250 seats. We were doing Cohan's *People Alone* and *People Together*. Some people thought these were wonderful works but they were not enough to fill even this little theatre – enough to make it pay. There was a company meeting at which Robin said the company was now going to "go to the top." He used those words so we made jokes about being based at the top of the Post Office tower. Shortly there after the company moved its seasons to the Sadlers Wells Theatre with some 1500 seats, a hugely ambitious thing from an administrator's point of view. It worked. There followed a period of success, in which quite large theatres were often sold out. Tickets were sold on the basis of the company's own choreographic work. Eventually this creativity dried up and then works like *Rooster* were needed to keep drawing in the public.

Yet this is currently a thriving building and you personally have an

artistically thriving company. Maybe we are wrong in thinking anything went wrong. You have to have the darkness before the dawn I
suppose.

RA: All art forms need a history; we haven't got a lot of it. The worrying
thing, as I said right at the beginning, is that something in the
infrastructure has gone, something has weakened. People outside the
world of Contemporary Dance might not understand the rights and
wrongs of a company no longer existing. They just see that the flagship,
which seemed to be the establishment, exists no longer. Rambert today
is not the same thing. A wide range of people were influenced by
seeing the particular kind of company that London Contemporary was.
Maybe because it was allowed to go badly wrong it had to close but I
think this weakened the field. I do. Its demise has confused people's
feelings about Contemporary Dance.

RM: I missed the significance of this point when you first raised it. It is an
important comment. Certainly there is no big fifty-two weeks a year
Contemporary Dance company working now as the LCDT did.

RA: There is Phoenix but it's a younger and smaller company.

RM: Yes but Phoenix, with the possible exception of when it was under
the direction of Neville Campbell, did not have a director who worked
through innovative material at a pre-rehearsal level or generated most
of its choreographic work out of its own people and processes.

RA: If you think of any one of the maybe twenty years of London
Contemporary, you can see people who are now out in the field in
all sorts of corners. There is Micha Bergese or Anthony Van Laast in the
commercial field or Charlotte (Kirkpatrick) who is teaching in your
school, or Darshan who is setting up his own company, Jonathan Lunn
who is now choreographing, Paul Douglas who went on to work with
Sue (a lot of people went on to work with Sue), or Kenny (Tharp) who
is doing so much education work up at Sadlers Wells. It's very
impressive that a company should have such a strong family feeling
and spread its influence so wide.

RM: I am trying to grasp your concept of an "infrastructure" which, as
you say, has been lost. This family did set up something national. There
were people with whom contact was made across the country. You
now have Veronica Lewis in an executive position here at The Place.
She was influenced and involved in the first Yorkshire residencies in
the 1970s. There were all these wonderful people around the country
whose energy was tapped by the LCDT. That is gone and no one has
got the muscle to do it anymore.

RA: It may be simplistic to say but the artistic director of the remaining
big company, Rambert, doesn't teach. One of Bob's extraordinary
strengths was this – what is now called "outreach". He had a way of
reaching out into the community in an influential way.

RM: And he did it himself; he did not have an outreach unit to do it as companies do now. He taught his dancers to do it, whether they liked it or not.

One item, which we have touched on already is that dance can transform people in ways more than physical. There was the idea that the most important thing was that the people in the company should be transformed in a special way. Do you think your life in dance has been transformative in that way at least partly because these people believed in this and they influenced you.

RA: I wouldn't disagree with that at all but it's hard for me to pinpoint who influenced this transformation. I think more and more that one of the extraordinary things about dance is that the material itself changes you. Just dealing with physical facts, dealing with finding out new things, being startled by new things which become clearer through teaching, through having to make it clear to someone who has no idea what they are doing. Bob came from a world where that was an accepted part of the work process. This was a tremendous influence on me and I feel in a strange transitional place. I know I've seen things younger people have never witnessed. Now, the whole thing has become so economically difficult and everything so transient even though there are miraculous new ways of working. All these new things have their own excitement.

Bob and his company were the first example I saw of dancers who grew closer to each other through the ongoing work of developing a company. This seemed to me quite vital. I don't say everyone should do it, but it's one of the reasons I work the way I do.

I'm intrigued that, after quite some deliberation, I keep choosing young people for my company, whether they are from our school or your school. I think that is part of this interest in growth. I quite understand someone like Sue who says she wants to have mature artists. I love that idea and yet I'm intrigued that when I consider people from all over the spectrum of dance, and all levels of experience I often choose a young dancer. It's the right thing for the company and for the way I work, seeing someone really grow up before my eyes.

I saw this at Rambert. As soon as someone who had a strong role as a company member moved on, someone magically took their place. Nothing was said, somebody suddenly grew up overnight. Perhaps someone who had been one of the wild ones – out late at the pub – suddenly became the one responsible for teaching the others. That is a process Robin very much believed in. He loved what he saw Bob do, because Bob achieved that with dancers. It is really significant that up until Bob left LCDT, there was a group of dancers who had been there for such a long time.

RM: One of the joys of running a school is that you see, not just choreography, but people becoming through it. That you are so interested in this seems to put you in Cohan's area of interest. You are not just turned on by your own choreography, but because dancers acquire a "becomingness" through it. I think this shows in your company. Cohan told me that people used to come, not just to see the choreography, but also to see the development of the people in the company. The dancers made manifest in dance the change they were going through.

RA: It's hard to talk about LCDT, to speak honestly about something that disappeared without sounding like one is dismissing or knocking it. When I was asked to come back here, it was a very important part of my job to make something positive out of a damaged situation, a damaged organization. Certainly in my first years after coming back it was quite hard. I knew that people who had been my friends in the company were very upset and angry, but I could not be part of that. It wasn't right. I was asked to come here not only because I was like an old friend, but also because I had a real interest in the future and in making some sort of bridge. I very much believe in John Ashford.[2] It's very significant that it was Robin who brought John here. John has had such a tremendous influence on the whole spectrum of dance in this country and provided the chance for so many young people to grow and make work. I come from a different corner of the dance field but we both respect each other and it's a good balance. I'm very happy about the potential and the plans for The Place and I think Robin would have understood. He would have been excited too.

## Notes

1. The Place Theatre
2. Director of The Place Theatre.

# Musical Dance and the Profound: An Interview with Robert North

Ross McKim

At: The Peacock Theatre, London
On: 8 October 1998

RM: What was there about the work of the LCDT that influenced the dance world around it?

RN: The first thing that comes to mind is a level of professionalism, a way of working that you don't often see in opera houses and in other dance companies; the fact that people were almost never injured and very rarely off; the fact that people worked very hard and in a very committed way (which is not what I see in the opera houses I work in around the world); the commitment to the work; the way Bob [Cohan] taught us we should work – he got a lot of that from Martha [Graham].

RM: You have worked with great big companies and very good ones. It appears that this attitude and commitment do not always exist in highly competent companies. How did the LCDT get that attitude?

RN: Graham was very professional, but economically you had to be with a small company. As you know from the ones you had, in small companies you have to lay the lino and put up the lights yourself. In the LCDT we occasionally had to do that. It was a smaller company, which was great. At maximum, we were eighteen or twenty.

RM: When I first joined we were fourteen.

RN: In a large company you have to portion out what you do much more, but with eighteen we were dancing all the time.

The LCDT was a small group of soloists. It was not a company with a star and a *corps de ballet* or a star, soloists and *corps de ballet*. This gave a different kind of responsibility. When I go to work with different companies I want that standard. But I now ask myself, "Why are you expecting this high standard? These people have been brought up with an entirely different mentality." For example, in Verona they want to

43

**Figure 9**
**Robert North, Paula Lansley in** *Place of Change.* **Choreography, Robert Cohan.**
**Photo: Anthony Crickmay. Courtesy of V&A Picture Library.**

do four hours work a day. They think more than that is excessive. We
did at least six and a half in the LCDT didn't we?[1]

RM: We didn't count.

RN: That's what I mean.

RM: Were we getting something back from the LCDT which dancers
don't often get?

RN: We were there to work and we enjoyed it. We got tired and we grumbled, but we enjoyed it. A disciplined work ethic was taught but it did not need to be enforced. Everyone wanted to do it. Mop told me it started to change near the end.[2] People got into the unions and they had to have breaks at the right time and so on.

Then there were Bob's very high artistic standards. You hear me now talking very nicely about Bob's high standards now; I used to bitch about him so much (laughter). I was bitching about something else. It was not the artistic standards, it was something else he was focusing on. He had different ideas from me and he wanted to do things I didn't want to do.

RM: We all bitched, maybe not everyone as much as you. Now look back on it all with a golden glow. When did you leave?

RN: I left after fifteen years. That was about '81.

RM: You needed Cohan for someone to rub up against, someone to disagree with.

RN: Towards the last five years, yes. Not for the first ten years. Then I followed everything he said word for word.

My actual criticism was that there finally became too much emphasis on a sort of physicality that leads to a kind of gymnastics. Physicality does not have to be so. For me the question was how to be musical and, finally, what is dancing? I felt that all around us, not just in the LCDT, dancing was disappearing. It was disappearing in ballet and in everything. People still called it dancing, but it had become this other activity.

RM: In the most successful days of the LCDT, apart from some of your pieces, there were few works set to musical scores. The most notable exception for Cohan was *Stabat Mater*. Richard [Alston] did music-based work. But for the most part there were pieces to sound effects and to rhythms but seldom to what we conventionally think of as music.

RN: Bob was interested in dynamic, dramatic musicality, but not so much in what I call dance musicality. He was more interested in theatrical movement rather than what I am calling dancing. Perhaps I should not say exactly what he was into, but this seems so to me.

RM: As *Cell* was almost "physical theatre."

RN: Yes, exactly. What I wanted to do was that thing called dancing. The motor starts to run and something else happens. For me Fred Astaire was always the best example . . . all those kind of people. That's why I like folk dancing and Flamenco. It does something different from what I will call "theatrical dance." I'm not against theatrical dance; I use it all the time. But I think at some time dance should start to rock.

RM: Much of the LCDT's work was based on Graham. There is a case cited somewhere of a confrontation between Fokine and Martha

Graham where he says dance is properly about happiness and joy ". . . and your dance Madame is about  . . ."

RN: ". . . darkness," and she says, ". . . it all comes from the solar plexus," and he says, ". . . no it doesn't" (laughter). But she danced. Martha loved to dance but she loved theatre so much that it appeared she was more interested in that. Martha's stuff was full of dancing. You always danced at some point or other in a Martha dance.

RM: Jane Dudley said to me that in the earlier concerts there was always a "dancey" piece first.

RN: That's interesting. Well *Diversions* (of Angels) is pretty "dancey." It's a bit square or what ever you want to call it. *Acrobats of God* was full of dancing. She always had at least one piece in a programme that was full of dancing when I was there.

RM: There seems to be a unique experience that arises through dance. It may be a bit different in different kinds of dance. Still this experience, in all dance that generates it, is not the same as the excitement that comes through other extreme physical acts like athletics. Mary Wigman began building a technique, not so much, it seems, to do things more skillfully, but beyond that to provide a special experience through dance (Wigman, 1996: 52). Then Curt Sachs says "all dance is ecstatic" (Sachs, 1933 [1937]). That might seem a bit over the top, but much dance does give you a special experience you could call "ecstasy."

RN: Yes. Something clicks off in your head and you say "that's dancing" in a special sense. That kind of dancing gets treated in a very poor way. Its treated as old fashioned. It's called clichéd. We say, "we all know how to do that," but we don't. It is very hard to do. It's called unoriginal. Well of course it's unoriginal. Dancing is very unoriginal. To find some new weird movement can seem very original but the minute you start dancing people say "old fashioned." So everybody avoids it. There are only a few steps that people will still use. One of them, I don't know why, is *coupé jeté*. It's in every technique in the world, but any other kind of fast foot work. . . .

If you watch Fred Astaire you can name some of the steps. You can't name them all, but you can certainly call them "steps." Michael Jackson is another great example. He is dancing.

A lot of it is wrapped up in steps. The steps give you the rhythm. Probably a lot of rhythmic dances were step dances originally. If you don't have steps and step moves, like tap dance moves, then there is a big element of dancing missing. In almost all folk dancing there is a lot of stepping. But again people avoid it because it looks old fashioned. It looks like the Rumba so sophisticated choreographers say, "Oh no, I can't do that." But people adore the Tango and Flamenco and will watch it forever. It's like Irish dancing which is popular now. All this stuff is essentially dancing.

RM: In a sense Ballet crystallized in the eighteenth and nineteenth centuries.[3] It might be argued that it did so much informed by the crystallization of Western musical forms which took place slightly earlier as, for example, in the work of Bach, Mozart and Beethoven. But there is, for example, African music which has very complex rhythms. It could be said to make European music of recent centuries look rhythmically unsophisticated.

RN: Belinda Quirey says the difference between African music and our music is the melody line.[4] We phrase music in a certain way. It's not so important that we do every beat. She says this phrasing is as in a "carole" or line dance where the phrase is the thing. In African music and dance, what is important is what you do on those beats . . . how you are moving your back and stomping your feet.

RM: In Mozart slow movements and elsewhere, there is an emphasis on melodies that soar over a harmonic structure and harmonic rhythm that does not have drive in the same way that much African percussion based music does. Such melody, if you dance to it, provokes a certain flowing quality in dancing and a specific experience of dancing.

RN: Yes exactly and you can see a pas de deux to it right away. Both these approaches, European and African come under what I call musical movement. They both give you the dance sensation.

RM: So through this musical dance is possibly a "dance sensation" we could call ecstasy akin to that generated by a Mozartian melody, or the melody of a songster like Schubert. But there is also another quality of ecstasy available in dance built on African, rhythmically based music.

RN: Yes, rhythms and melodies like that get in your body and you want to move around to them. The better they are the more you do. We say: "That's my song I can dance to that."

RM: You have choreographed to both these kinds of music. You have choreographed, for example, to Schubert, which is melodically based and to Flamenco which is largely rhythmically based.

RN: We played music all the time, you and I, when we were in the LCDT.[5] The company did not, however, demonstrate its musicality through its choreographed works. That's why I did *Troy Game*. I think the dancers in the company were musical and they could all bop at a party. When I went to Rambert and Bob asked me what I wanted to do, I said, "I want it to be more musical. I want it all to be about music and what that is." He said: "You mean like Jiri Kylian – more classical?" I said, "No," but I couldn't give an example then. At Rambert I tried very hard to get people to use music musically. Kylian is musical; so is Christopher [Bruce], so are Jerry Robbins and Balanchine, and so is Ashton.

   In a way I like Frederick Ashton the best because he is simpler with it. The others tend sometimes to get very elaborate and complicated.

It's all on the music and it all works but Fred would just do what the music said and not fight it. My particular love is the lyrical things that Frederick Ashton did. Jerry Robbins did such things too. I just found him exquisite. I did not think we should lose that.

I remember having a conversation with Bill Louther quite early on. He said if he had a school he would have everyone learn to play a musical instrument. I said I thought that Bob was trying to do the opposite, that he wanted to go against musicality. Bill was very musical; Bob was also very musical but he wanted to use theatre musicality, dramatic musicality, not musicality dictated by a piece of music.

RM: That is in the Graham tradition and he danced with her for twenty-one years.

RN: Yes. Louis Horst, for example, would write music at the same time as Martha made the dance. But she often had the music and choreographed to it. I think what Bob wanted to do was to choreograph the dance and then have someone write the music on top. That's what he did with *Masque of Separation*, which I thought worked very well.

Of course, if you do a lot of this musical dancing I am talking about, people get very bored. You can't do a lot of it.

RM: You earn a living by making it not boring.

RN: I always try to put a lot of dancing in to whatever I do; but more and more I try and fill it up with something else that you can follow. Like a Fred Astaire movie in which there are little moments of brilliant dancing – that's not what I do, it's what he does. There is a long story line that takes you with it.

The great thing that Antony Tudor did was to mix up the dancing with the story line in a way that had not been done before. In *Petipa* you do the mime to tell the story and then you do a little dance. Apparently he had a very clear idea about what the dance should mean in every place but it still looks like dance and story are separate. Tudor tried to dance out the situation; Jerry Robbins did too in some of his things. *Dances at a Gathering* is very clearly concerned with competition or flirtation. He is dancing the dramatic situation and the story line, so it's very easy to keep watching. If you just do abstract dancing for a long time it's very hard not to wander. I mean I wander.

RM: How about the training. You and I went to the Royal Ballet School. The next time I saw you, you were in the Graham Company. How did her physical, theatrical dance training affect the way you experienced movement?

RN: I got into Martha's company because I had been in the London Contemporary Dance School here. Bob helped me get into Martha's company.

Concerning Ballet and Modern Dance, I remember having a discussion with Bob and Noemi (Lapzeson). I said, ". . . that reminds me of this ballet movement." So I got up and did this ballet movement and Noemi said, ". . . yuch!" (laughter). I said, "no you are wrong; this is a beautiful movement. It's not wrong just because its Ballet. . . ."

RM: So some Modern Dancers may have rejected the dance musicality you are interested in because it looks like ballet or is associated with ballet.

RN: Martha wanted to go, like Picasso, to the primitive. She wanted to get away from eighteenth-century taste. But I think we are seeing now that a lot of seventeenth- and eighteenth-century taste is good. Because some of it was very flowery doesn't mean the structure underneath it wasn't terrific. It was. So much ballet was about joy and light, like the impressionists. Modern Dance had to be the opposite, so it became heavy. That's fine, but I don't think you should throw the other out.

RM: Did you get any more musical or any more able to dance musically through Graham training?

RN: I think so. If you have good teachers they insist that you put the music way inside you. They insisted you work very deeply with the music. Gene MacDonald was, for me, the most musical teacher at the Graham studio, but there were other ones. It became less and less but at that point there was an emphasis on musicality. They had very good pianists.

Bob liked us to be accurate with whatever music or sound was used. We worked for hours in this way on *Cell*. It has basically a sound track rather than a musical score.

RM: In classes Bob was very careful about the use of rhythm and rhythmic patterns. For example, he would build a five in which each beat would be determined by a gesture or step. That is a case of steps making a phrase of five.

RN: But that kind of thing doesn't rock.

RM: Why were you attracted to the Martha Graham Company and to LCDT?

RN: I really liked doing the technique although I wasn't loose, and you usually think of Graham Technique as needing that. The technique suited me in its physicality. It's easier to get a hold of than ballet. Ballet is so fiendishly difficult.

RM: I was, if anything, over-loose and had trouble with ballet because of that. I could get away with doing it while feeling sort of disconnected. Cohan's technique and teaching could put you in connection with your physicality.

RN: It taught you where the muscles were and how you connected them all up. Ballet often teaches you the steps. There is the hope that somewhere along the way you will learn to connect your body up.

Good ballet teaching will connect you up but generally you just learn the steps.

RM: I danced ballet best when I was in doing classes with Katie Croften.[6] She didn't say that much.

RN: It was her class that was so good. The exercises taught you how to get down deep into the muscle. It was her musicality too. She insisted on it.

RM: Regarding this term, "deep physicality," we at Rambert School had the Council for Dance Education and Training come and complain that "depth" of physicality was an invalid term within our assessment criteria. I had carefully put the word in quotation marks in documentation. They said you can't talk about "depth" of physicality, but the term's use is important. It is something Cohan got at, but I don't remember if he used the word.

RN: It's one of the first things he got at. He got you way down to the muscle close to the bones rather than the muscles just on the surface. You had to work with that kind of (he demonstrates in his chair) . . . I'm imitating Cohan the moment I try to do it. He would get you deep into muscles you don't use when you do ballet badly.

RM: Ballet is beautiful but has some nasty temptations in it. There can be a superficial lightness which is a point of departure for ballet parody. This is far from the way, for example, Nureyev danced when he was young. It was from deep in the muscles and yet he moved softly and, in a sense, lightly.

RN: A lot of stuff Modern Dance got back to is really in ballet. Good ballet teachers talk about it. Really good ballet dancers do use the floor as you are taught to do in a Modern Dance class and as Nureyev used it. There is a kind of projection that comes through when you work that way.

RM: You were always interested in teachers and in teaching. You had many guest teachers when you directed Rambert Dance Company. You had a lot to do with Matt Mattox coming to teach us at the LCDT when you were associate choreographer there.[7]

RN: Yes I was interested in figuring it out.

RM: You went to the Royal Ballet School when I did. It was thought to be the best school around, but you were unhappy.

RN: I didn't have very good teachers. I thought Katie [Croften] was the end of the world, so if anyone said anything the opposite of Katie I hated it. It wasn't a high standard of teaching when we were at the Royal. You had had a lot of teaching already but I had to learn good information. I was being taught a lot of junk.

RM: It was hard to find something meaningful in it.

RN: Well, it was very superficial. Katie was deep; Bob was deep. Katie was also very connected to the past. Bob was . . . Martha was looking for . . . the primitive. She was trying to get back to something way back before ballet, to mythical sources. They were all looking for something more intelligent.

RM: There was a sense or awareness around that building, around The Place, that something intelligent was going on.

RN: There were some bright people. At the very least they were trying.

RM: You tend to miss that the rest of your life.

RN: You do. Dancers don't have to be bright, but there were a very bright group of people there. You got that stimulus too. Not just the stimulus of seeing good dancers, a lot of bun heads. They were intelligent. They were trying to adopt an intelligent approach to dance. They were thinking about it and that is good.

Whenever you start off something new you tend to attract a lot of talented people. A lot of talented people did come to The Place at that time. Later it created lots of good dancers, good bodies, but the people were not as creative as they had been earlier. There was also that initial boom of choreographers. I don't know if they will ever amount to anything but it was exciting.

RM: When I first joined the LCDT is was a pretty unusual group of bodies and a pretty unusual group of people. It was not a big establishment. It was known but it was not the world famous company it came to be later on when we were in it.

RN: It was a strong group of Modern Dancers with a couple of ballet people in there like Linda [Gibbs] and you and, I guess, me a little bit. The ballet element maybe made it more refined. It resulted in people pointing their feet a little bit.

RM: Informing Bob's way of running the company there seemed to be a Grotowski-like idea that the process of work was as important as the product. The process of making the performance was as important as that performance itself. There was even the thought that the product, or performance, would take care of itself if the process was good. You might not go along with that. You might have thought Cohan was over the top in talking about how dancers were working on their deeper selves.

RN: I made fun of it but I thought that was right.

RM: Really?

RN: Yes, yes, I thought, "you can change yourself." But I was always interested in dancing so I was interested in changing yourself to dance not changing how you thought. It was just a difference of emphasis. Your work should have something profound about it, not just something superficial.

What was missing at The Place, for me, was dancing. What was missing in some Modern Dance was dancing. Paul Taylor did dancing. Merce did a kind of dancing. Alvin Ailey did dancing. I once thought his work was too close to musicals but now I think I might change my mind. The whole dance world was shifting off dancing; and dancing was why I wanted to do it. I loved dancing.

RM: With a seriousness, or some kind of profundity, which was equal to what Bob and other people were getting. They were not, however, primarily concerned with dancing in the sense that you use the word.

RN: Yes.

## References

Sachs, C. (1963 [1937]) *The World History of the Dance.* New York: W W Norton.

Wigman, M. (1996) *The Language of Dance,* Middlestown. Connecticut: Weslyan University Press.

## Notes

1. North is talking about rehearsal time as this takes place in addition to class and performance time.
2. Janet Eager, Administrative Director of the LCDT was known as "Mop."
3. It seems fair to make this claim in that the ballet technique Carlo Blasis codified in a book in 1820 contains the basis of the Ballet technique of today. Furthermore, the famous ballet "classics" like *Giselle, La Sylphide, Swan Lake* and *The Sleeping Beauty* are all of the nineteenth century.
4. Belinda Quirey is an expert in historical European dance.
5. Robert North plays guitar very well, particularly Flamenco guitar. We used to play flute and guitar pieces when on tour. Other company members sang in some of these sessions. Groups of us would drum together.
6. Kathleen Croften danced with Pavlova as a soloist.
7. Matt Maddox, an important Jazz Dance teacher, danced in many New York musicals. He particularly based his teaching on that of Jack Cole.

# Dancing with Siobhan Davies/Awareness and Robin Howard: An Interview with Sean Feldman

Ross McKim

At: the Interviewer's home
On: 12 September 1998

RM: You went to the London School of Contemporary Dance from 1983 to 1986 when the London Contemporary Dance Theatre was still in place. If there was any significant influence from that company on you as a dancer, a teacher and as a choreographer, what was it?

SF: During the three years I was at the school Jane Dudley was still the director. She was Graham-based as was Robert Cohan. Probably the most significant influence on me from that time was the passion Jane put into her teaching and into us as students. It's difficult to know how to describe Jane's class. She was certainly quite tough with us. She was very demanding at times; but she always encouraged such a sense of beauty and elegance in the movement that it lifted you up somehow. It was also very inspiring having the company around and watching them rehearse. The dancers were so articulate and sensitive that it deepened my sense of what dance could be.

RM: Cohan, he spoke of how people used to come, not just to see the choreography of the LCDT, but to see the dancers who seemed to be having a special experience. There appears to have been something that came through Cohan and Jane Dudley which was not just Graham. It was the almost religious enthusiasm they transferred. Did you guys experience that in the school?

SF: Yes we did and maybe that's why I felt so inspired by Jane. If I think about some of the dancers who were at the school then, they were clearly inspired to move in a way that took them beyond technique and beyond themselves in every way. Because of this they went on to become such wonderful performers.

RM: People say there has been influence on dance now from the LCDT

**Figure 10**
**Anthony Van Laast, Kate Harrison in *Forest*. Choreography, Robert Cohan.**
**Photo: Anthony Crickmay. Courtesy of V&A Picture Library.**

but no one seems to put a finger on it. A number of choreographers have made enduring dances in the style of Graham or Cunningham but I think it is less easy to claim that many people went on to choreograph enduring work in the style of the LCDT.

You were trained in the fairly heavy Graham training of that time. Now you do something less heavy. I know the word "heavy" is not a very good one. Is there anything you got from that training that you put in your teaching now?

SF: There's a lot from my training that's still very useful to me, as a dancer and teacher. The Graham training focused a lot on the breath; part of what I do now is geared towards having a greater awareness of breath in the way that I move. I still like to work both through parallel and turned out positions to extend the articulation of the legs or use the depth of my plié to explore how far I can shift my weight in space. These ideas, and actually a great deal of what I gained as a student, are still there in the way that I work these days.

RM: You do "Release" but you do a very physical "Release" perhaps because you are getting at what Cohan and Dudley were getting at in a different way.

SF: In some ways, Jane and the other teachers I had as a student taught me to move from as deeply within me as I could. The work that I do now also explores movement that comes from deep in the body. So both the Graham work and the Release-based work move towards developing an expressive and articulate instrument. What differs is the information given and then, as a result, the experience of the movement. So it looks quite different.

RM: Did Cohan teach you often?

SF: No, not so much. He taught occasionally while I was still a student at the school and then again when I took company classes.

RM: When did you first work with Siobhan Davies?

SF: I started working with Sue in '92. Before that I spent a while dancing with several companies including Janet Smith and Dancers. With Janet I learned a lot about being fluid and connected as a dancer. One of the wonderful things about working with Sue and the other dancers in her company is just how much further I've found myself exploring this. Sue will often get us to question ourselves about how the movement ought to be done. From this questioning there is a wonderful search and discovery process for the physicality of the movements. It's great to be curious about the work in this way. Little by little, over the years, this has not only changed the way I move but also fed me more knowledge and understanding about movement.

RM: Robin Howard and Cohan, but perhaps particularly Robin, had the idea that they would found a company which would use American Modern Dance but that they would also base its work on what Robin called "love". One of the things I remember about working with Sue, when she was still dancing, was that whenever she was injured she would start taking care of everybody else. She was sensitive to every body else. Is she still like that?

SF: Yes, she is very much like that. I think Sue is mostly concerned, when we are working, that we take care of ourselves. If you're injured Sue will check to see that you're getting the treatment you need. She is also sensitive to the dancers being tired, if it's been a particularly long and difficult day. Sue is very like that.

RM: Cohan was interested in his dancers as they developed as people as well as artists. Sue is also interested in the dancers as people.

SF: I think Sue's work is partly fuelled by getting to know her dancers as people. She is interested in how we feel about all sorts of things. We will often go off on a tangent in rehearsal and end up discussing something else together.

RM: Cohan was interested in people and what they can bring to the work, but he was not known for taking more mature dancers into his company. Sue does this because of what they can bring to the work. People go off and have babies and then come back. She does not get rid of them because they have babies.

SF: The opposite. She embraces that. Sue enjoys working with dancers she knows well and she encourages the dancers who've had babies to come back when they are ready. Sue has two children of her own and so, when the needs of a young family mean a dancer can't come in one day, then she is immediately understanding and just gets on with the other dancers.

RM: Bob was concerned with awareness, and indeed awaking from a waking sleep is a concept he took from Gurdjieff. Sue seems very aware. She had, when I worked with her, an uncanny ability to know how you were feeling.

SF: It seems to me that Sue is very perceptive of people and she is always very considerate towards their needs and well-being. I think it's probably because Sue is down to earth that she's sensitive to the dancer's feelings in this way.

RM: Someone pointed out to me that Cohan tried to do a new thing with each work. This, of course, is fraught with danger. You have said Sue does much the same thing. She does not find a successful style and stick with it.

SF: No she doesn't. If the style comes from anywhere, it comes from the dancers. It is about how we interpret the work and also the training we do together as a group. We are all so individual in our movement that even then it is difficult to say that this one thing is the Sue Davies style. I think the constant in Sue's work is the depth to which we research the movement material and the different qualities we can bring to it. There is always a richness in the work.

RM: Cohan had a big influence on his company through teaching class. Sue doesn't teach.

SF: Our classes are usually taught by members of the company with occasional guest teachers like Scott Clark and Jeremy Nelson. Sue's teaching really comes in rehearsal and in the notes she gives once we're performing. In this way Sue is a wonderful teacher. She gets to know how we move, how we like to do things and she uses this knowledge to challenge us further.

RM: Cohan was very concerned with process. There is the Grotowski model. He gave up performance because it mucked up the experience of rehearsal, of process, because everyone was too concerned with the show. That became a big problem with the LCDT because they had to perform so much. One of Cohan's complaints is that the LCDT got so successful that they had to produce six works a year, and maybe even twelve, in very little rehearsal time. There is this thought that if the process – the rehearsal and class experience – is healthy then the performance almost takes care of itself. Sue works quite a long time to make a piece.

SF: Usually about eight or nine weeks. The trend recently in Holland and Belgium is to take even longer, three to six months to make new work. I have a friend, Mark Haim in New York, who took a couple of years over a solo programme. It seems to me that process time is definitely valued much more these days.

When we are making a new piece with Sue we spend the first couple of weeks just exploring and playing with the ideas Sue has for the work. More often than not we will throw away a lot of what comes up during this time. I think Sue finds this time very useful and also necessary. It helps find the nature of the piece and it definitely helps us get into different ways of moving.

RM: All that takes time. There are claims that the LCDT burned out because it had so little process time. Sue does not work all year round. She not only has a home life she has a life life. How many months does she tend to work?

SF: In general the dancers work for about six months over two periods in the year. Usually three to four months in the spring, rehearsing and making work before going on tour and then another tour in the autumn with a shorter rehearsal period of about four weeks. Sue works through the year, sometimes making work for other companies and often spending time in the office when we are not in rehearsal.

RM: The LCDT worked all year round and toured some twenty-six weeks a year with, in my time, eight performances a week. Sue's method gives the dancers time to go off and do other things.

SF: Sue's company works in this way partly because of financial restraints, having just so much money to employ the dancers for a certain amount of time each year. When we are not working with Sue we usually try to find work elsewhere for a while either teaching or dancing with other choreographers. I think it works well though to have this time away. It can be quite inspiring just being in a different environment for a while. The dancers that have children get more time with them. I also think the work benefits from these breaks as a fresher energy comes back into it.

RM: Is there anything else you want to say?

SF: Yes – you mentioned Robin Howard. He is someone else who inspired me very much when I was at the school.

RM: In what way did he affect you?

SF: During my second year as a student a few of us used to spend Friday afternoons with Robin. He was interested in the students' personal development and he took this time to talk with us about our thoughts, feelings and general well-being. His interest was in a form of personal development called psycho-synthesis. Our time together as a group was not really that structured. He would just encourage us to be open about expressing ourselves in whatever way we felt we needed to or was appropriate to us individually and as a group.

RM: Did he manifest any theory of his own in these sessions?

SF: Not that I can remember or ever knew. Maybe he did. I think Robin was mainly concerned that the course offered us as much support for our personal development, as people not just dancers, as possible. He felt that was important and this was one way of providing that.

RM: I think that was called, "Robin's course".

SF: Yes it was really Robin's course. The rest of the training was very demanding. I found this time with Robin helped me get a better perspective on it and of what I wanted from it. It was wonderful to have that kind of support and insight. Robin wanted us to be aware of each other and ourselves. I've often felt that helped me take time and try to be more sensitive in my dancing.

Figure 11
Paula Lansley, Ross McKim in *Khamsin*. Choreography, Robert Cohan.
Photo: Anthony Crickmay. Courtesy of V&A Picture Library.

# The Development of the Northern School
# Of Contemporary Dance and its Links with
# the London Contemporary Dance Theatre

Alison Beckett

The first outreach activity by the London Contemporary Dance Theatre (LCDT) in the early 1970s was to Yorkshire. Robert Cohan agreed to choreograph a work while in residence at Bretton Hall and allow young people from the area to watch the process. It was a stressful experience for the company members who felt that they should be on their best behaviour under such close scrutiny, but a brilliant one for the youngsters who were able to watch their dance heroes at work. The piece produced was *Khamsin*, which became a piece of repertory for the company and latterly was given to The Northern School of Contemporary Dance by Cohan and has been revived by the students several times during the life of the School.

Among the children attending the residency were a group from Harehills Middle School (an inner-city school in Leeds), who, under the guidance of their dedicated Physical Education teacher, Nadine Senior, had been given the opportunity to learn to dance as part of their P.E. curriculum. Dance had achieved such a high profile in the school thanks to the effort of this teacher supported by the headmaster, Jack Bramwell, that the children were serious and committed and regarded their participation in the dance work of the school as a great privilege. Many of the children were from ethnic minorities and were able to develop their innate talent so that their school performances were of an exceptionally high standard and the youth group which grew out of the school's dance activity quickly gained a national reputation.

The interest that Robin Howard had in bringing Contemporary Dance to Britain, and in making it more generally accessible through tours and residencies, served to promote educational interest in and LCDT and particularly inspired the young dancers at Harehills. A special hero of the children was Namron, a founder member of the company, and being

West Indian, he served as a valued role model to the boys who were mainly from African-Caribbean and Asian backgrounds.

Latterly Namron and other members of the company visited Harehills to teach and give workshops whenever they toured the North, and strong links between LCDT and Harehills were formed. In the meantime, these highly talented and motivated young people were seeking training for a career in dance and as they reached school-leaving age they set off to audition for the London Contemporary Dance School where they found considerable success in their dance studies. They had greater problems, however, coping with living in London with all the pressures and temptations of the big city. Jane Dudley, who was at that time Director of the School, called upon Namron more than once to try to sort out one or other of the Harehills students who had got into trouble or was failing to adjust to life at the LCDS.

Nadine Senior watched the progress of her protégés with interest and concern and whilst she delighted in their success (and it has to be said that they were, almost without exception, heading for significant careers in dance) she was concerned about those who were dropping out because they had failed to cope with the demands of London life.

The obvious answer was to offer some sort of vocational training program in the North to enable these young people to train in a more sheltered environment, where the transition to professional discipline would be supported by an educational approach. This idea, once germinated, became the seed that flowered into the Northern School Of Contemporary Dance.

Using the LCDS as a model, a training program was developed by a small team led by Nadine Senior, supported by funding from the Gulbenkian Foundation and Leeds City Council. This placed the NSCD firmly in the maintained sector which has proved enormously beneficial to its development. The College now enjoys the status of being a College of Higher Education affiliated to the University of Leeds. Its links with the London School have gradually become more tenuous as the NSCD has matured and reached self-sufficiency.

There is no doubt, however, that the influence of those early pioneering days of the LCDT remains evident in the work and philosophy of the College and some of the staff who founded it are still working with its students. Namron, who was a founder lecturer, taught Contemporary technique until very recently. Nina Fonaroff, who was involved in the early development of LCDS, is still in a consultancy role for the Choreography course at the NSCD which is led by her protégé from LCDS, Debbie Johnson. Sharon Donaldson and Gurmit Hukam, were both Harehills children and Gurmit was involved in the original residency. Sharon trained at LCDS, danced with Phoenix and is now a full-time lecturer in Contemporary Dance at the College.

Gurmit Hukam was also a founder lecturer and taught Contemporary technique for several years. He took a break to become rehearsal director for Phoenix Dance Company and then to run the very successful HND in dance at Newcastle College. He returned to the College in 1995 as Artistic Director and Head of Contemporary Dance Studies. Nadine Senior, who has ben Principal of the College since it opened in 1985, has announced that she will be retiring on 31 December 2001 and Gurmit Hukam is now the Principal designate.

The NSCD has developed and matured into a centre of excellence for the training and education of contemporary dancers with an impressive new building which is an extension of its original home in a disused synagogue in Leeds. It maintains, however, its links with the London Contemporary Dance Theatre through the staff it employs and the philosophy which underpins the curriculum. Several ex-dancers, such as Darshan Singh Bhuller, his wife Sally Estep and Philip Taylor still have close associations with the NSCD.

**Figure 12**
Micha Bergese, Ross McKim in *Masque of Separation*. Choreography, Robert Cohan.
Photo: Anthony Crickmay. Courtesy of V&A Picture Library.

Changes in choreographic approaches to both movement and expression have moved the art form some considerable distance from those pioneering years. As the NSCD moves confidently into the 21st Century, it continues to foster creativity and invention in its students. The roots of practice remain, however, firmly established in the seminal work of London Contemporary Dance Theatre.

November 2001

# London Contemporary Dance Theatre: Its Legacy in Higher Education in the UK

Janet Adshead-Lansdale

I trace the flowering of an American form of contemporary dance in the UK in the late 1960s, through the 1970s and into the early 1980s. The evolution of London Contemporary Dance Theatre was timely, I argue, in meeting the changing needs of dance within both the theatrical and educational contexts of this period. The subsequent tensions that arose in the relationship between this form of dance, the professional theatre and dance education worlds, are articulated. An explanation for the rapid rise and fall of the company is constructed within the frame of rapidly changing cultural positions.

KEYWORDS: London Contemporary Dance Theatre, Modern educational dance, Modern dance, British new dance, Dance education, Physical Education

## Introduction

In the UK in the late 1960s and early 1970s, a crucial shift in the art form of dance coincided with an equally crucial acknowledgement of dance in higher education, with far-reaching effects. A "window of opportunity" presented itself which, knowingly or not, the London Contemporary Dance Theatre was perfectly placed to exploit. By the same token here lay the seeds of its extraordinarily rapid downfall.

To support such an argument it is necessary to explore the evolution of theatre dance and of dance education since the late 1960s with reference to the wider European and North American contexts. Critically, the purpose is to hold these two, sometimes rather separate, fields of human endeavor in relationship and debate the manner of their interaction at a time of major changes. I follow a loosely chronological structure, tracking the way dance education evolved in the early twentieth century alongside the emergence of early forms of modern dance. The main part of this paper recounts the subsequent flowering of a form of Contemporary Dance in the theatre in partnership with the growth of academic qualifications in dance at both school and university levels. A history is constructed of the growth of the London Contemporary Dance Theatre, which explains its educational impact. This complex relationship is compounded by simultaneous changes in the dance theatre world towards postmodernist forms. Finally some of the reasons for the precipitate demise of the company, although its work in education still continues to have significance, are articulated.[1]

## Dance Education in the Early Twentieth Century: The Emergence of Modern Educational Dance

During the first half of the present century, the emphasis in dance education was on grace and poise (for girls only, of course) and on dance as a physical and social therapy (Layson, 1970). Grove's famous assertion (1895) that dance might not only brighten the mind of the backward child, but also effect beneficial changes of mood and encourage discipline, is typical of much of the late nineteenth and early twentieth-century literature both on education generally and on dance education in particular. The revival of interest in folk dance forms instigated by Cecil Sharp early in the twentieth century similarly emphasized the recreational, physical and social aspects of dance (Sharp, 1913; Kennedy, 1964).

Duncan's work in Europe in the 1920s had already begun to affect the art and education experiences of many students training to be teachers, although an infrastructure of the kind which the Laban followers later created was never evident. Teaching, although important to Duncan, was not her primary motive (see Layson, 1987; Daly, 1995). As the early twentieth century progressed, the dance curriculum became dominated by folk dance and by Duncan-derived modern dance forms such as Eurhythmics, Euchorics, Expression Gymnastics, Natural Movement, Margaret Morris Movement and the Revived Greek Dance.[2] These were some of the many new dance forms of the time, each claiming to be different from any other but sharing a critique of the prevailing theatre form (ballet) as too restrictive and ossified, unable to respond to the challenges of the modern world. They also shared an attitude to education that favored individual development and expression.[3] Taken together these forms affected dance education both in state and private schools and influenced all levels from primary education to higher education.[4]

At this time the rationale for the teaching of dance was that it contrasted with, and balanced, the supposedly real, and much more challenging, intellectual demands of the rest of the school curriculum. While this argument ensured a place for dance and gave it a certain credibility, it simultaneously constrained the form it might take. It curtailed its artistic and intellectual ambitions from the start. Only some forms of dance could fill these requirements. While the ground was prepared for the acceptance of an Expressionist dance form by both the Duncan-derived dance in the theatre and its companion educational developments, two very different factors facilitated its successful adoption throughout the education system at the end of World War II. One factor was Laban's emphasis on the power of movement as a mode of individual expression, and thus its compatibility with the expansion of child-centered notions of education.[5] The second, and much more practical factor which gave impetus to such change was the presence in the UK from the 1930s of some of the main protagonists as refugees from World War II.

After the war, texts were swiftly translated into English (Laban had begun publishing in 1920, but English texts first became available in 1947; then 1948; 1960). British writers' reworking and adapting of the material gave it direct application to the local scene and thus both validity and support (e.g. Preston-Dunlop, 1963; Russell, 1965, 1969). Laban's previous experience in Germany helped to make the organization of school activities and community movements a relatively straightforward matter.[6] A professional organization offered training courses for potential teachers through short courses, summer schools and full time courses. These were strongly supported by teacher training colleges and Local Education Authorities.[7] Although work that linked professional dancers to the formal education system had existed sporadically from the 1920s, even the Laban-based development did not bring a large-scale professional company directly into relationship with educators.[8] It was not, therefore, until the 1960s that dance company education work began to develop in a systematic way, prefiguring the subsequent methods and success of the London Contemporary Dance Theatre.[9]

It is not difficult to understand the attractiveness of the Laban movement to the educational world, given the lack of sympathy between the prevailing theatre form of ballet and the concurrent philosophy of education. The classical art forms and their linguistic manifestations (e.g. in the teaching of Latin and Greek) were in sharp decline. Ballet, the dance equivalent, had never been part of the wider school context and stood no chance of taking root at this moment despite its modernist inclinations in the same period.[10] In any event, Physical Education had no link with the classical arts except in the idealization of the male body through athletic activity – not a suitable role model for the education of girls at a time when it was important that they relinquish the freedoms of war-time and return to home life to ensure sufficient jobs for war veterans. Femininity and individual expressivity were more to the point.

The changing ecology and ethic of women's education is not irrelevant, since it is women who have pioneered and supported these dance developments throughout the twentieth century.[11] Despite the fact that Dance Education within the state-funded system of the 1960s placed great emphasis on its relevance for all young people, it was particularly attractive to young women. Its wider appeal was based on arguments about the "universality of movement forms," i.e. since mankind shares a common potential for moving, dance is of value; since movement is innate, everyone can enjoy dance; there is a beneficial psychological effect in experiencing a harmonious and balanced range of movement qualities;[12] and that opportunities for group interaction are maximized through dance, so enhancing socialization and social education. A new idea emerged, that dance can offer students an aesthetic experience with, potentially, the structure of an art form.

In this period, the late 1960s, immediately preceding the establishment of the Graham-derived form of modern dance through the London Contemporary Dance Theatre, "modern educational dance" became widely taught both in schools and in state-funded teacher training colleges. It appeared either under the umbrella of Expressive Arts or of Physical Education in primary schools, and within Physical Education in the secondary school curriculum. Thus it flourished because it answered some of the needs of those contexts, providing a child-centered, "creative" and "aesthetic" arm. What was significant in clinching the relationship between this particular form of modern dance and the education system was the consonance of the artistic and educational ideologies. This is a crucial factor in analyzing relationships between these two, sometimes quite distinct, sectors of the arts and education.

It is also clear from this particular development, and of equal relevance to the present, how easily and quickly the type of dance style adopted in the state education system can change. In less than twenty years it had mutated from naturalistic early modern dance and folk dance to heavily Expressionistic forms. The indeterminate and fluid character of modern educational dance, with its many synonyms (creative/expressive dance, among others) was partly its strength, since its precise character was less important than its flexibility and adaptability in contributing to the open and non-prescriptive aims of child development.

## Modern Dance in the Context of the UK Theater

The theatre world of dance across Europe and North America was itself in flux at this time. Just as the emergent British Ballet earlier in the century had owed much to Russia in its flowerings, British early modern dance drew from North American experience as well as Central European dance styles. Following quickly on the heels of both ballet and early modern dance developments in the 1930s, came Kurt Jooss's performances and Laban and Wigman's work. The Jooss Ballet based itself in England, and although it continued with its planned tours, leaving for the USA in 1939 for a highly successful three-year period, Jooss, with

Leeder, remained behind. The company then returned to England where the revival of works such as *The Green Table* and *The Big City* reinforced the European realist and Expressionist message.[13] The overlap of dates and locations of performances of these new dance styles, and the comprehensiveness of the spread of both ballet and modern dance across Europe, implies a closer relationship between genres than historians have sometimes suggested. In this sense neither the UK, nor its dance heritage is quite as insular as it is sometimes thought to be; the cultural interrelationships make interesting reading.

The departure of the Jooss company to Essen in 1951 deprived England of a major theatre form and in consequence cast the Laban inheritance in education adrift from its theatrical roots. It is ironic that by the late 1960s UK public performances of Expressionist modern dances had largely ceased, in the face of political complications for choreographers of German origin and a general antipathy to all things German. It was not until 1993 that a thorough-going study of Mary Wigman's work, which attempted to understand her relationship to the prevailing political context, was published (Manning, 1993). As Toepfer says of this text, it "exposes ambiguous political values embedded in American as well as German dance cultures" (1994: 189). Wigman's "exposure of politics" rather than their transcendence testifies to her contribution to a critique of the relationship between dance and (German) life.

Manning also points to the political necessity, for earlier historians of the period, of making a clean break between the arts and Nazi culture while Manning herself is able to undermine this break to suggest a much closer relationship between *Ausdruckstanz* and the political realities of the time. The writing of the history of American modern dance, which largely ignores the three tours made by Mary Wigman to the USA in the 1930s, Manning argues, denies its European inheritance.[14] Manning's analysis is persuasive and her 1990s rewriting of history with a greater political sensitivity is both a valuable corrective and a useful example for this reassessment of the British view of the London Contemporary Dance Theatre's contribution to dance.[15] As a European reader I have long been troubled by the a-political emasculation of dance of this period.

If all was not rosy in this post-war Expressionist world, waiting in the wings was the Graham-based form of modern dance, the American counterpart to the Central European movement. In its original form, nothing could be further from the refined aestheticism of the American modernist movement as exemplified by Clement Greenberg and his followers. Mark Franko's revisiting of the period in his text *Dancing Modernism/Performing Politics* (1995) attacks modernism's "continuous reduction to essentials culminating in irreducible 'qualities'" (p. ix) on the grounds that it obscures an understanding of the ideological base of modern dance. Franko also questions the received wisdom of modernism,

What this empirical approach ignored, while it courted scientific respectability, was the cultural context in which modern dance operates, i.e. that of art within the wider field of the cultural practices of Western European and North American society. An approach from the History of Art could offer, and would demand, a very different mode of enquiry from the History of Sport in its themes, obsessions, and explanations, even while they share a historical methodology.[28] It matters very much where dance is located on this spectrum. I argued then – and nearly twenty years experience since has not dissuaded me – that to understand a form which in character is primarily aesthetic, and often artistic, it is necessary to surround it with the history and critical practices of art forms, and of aesthetic experience, rather than regard it as an adjunct to sport (Adshead, 1980). Most important, this view has the value that the long-standing sleight of hand that equates dance with "movement" could finally be exposed and the importance of the codification of movement in different ways in different dance styles recognized.[29]

Thus, empirical study in dance was eschewed as a necessary compensation for the emphasis on scientific approaches as the shift took place from comprehensive degree courses in Physical Education (which included dance) to separate degree courses in Dance, in Human Movement Studies and in Sports Science (Adshead, 1980). Today, it might be viewed differently, and greater emphasis placed, for example, upon understanding what constitute safe working practices for the dancing body, based on empirical research; but a valuable conceptual change had been accomplished, in which dance is seen primarily as embedded in cultural and artistic practices rather than as recreational and predominantly physical endeavor.[30]

A further confusion, however, in the midst of this period of rapid change lay in the dilemma about what sort of dance students should study. If Modern Educational Dance was losing currency and Modern Dance in its Central European form barely existed as artistic practice, what should take its place? It can be advantageous to be vague about the character of the dance taught, and Laban's supposedly "style-free" form of dance was an attractive, if improbable and unconvincing, proposition. However, it leaves unanswered the question of the value that could be attributed to a form of dance that seemed to have no connection with the external world. This was the kind of question that I, and other theorists of the time, asked, arguing that reference to a public world of dance and to a shared critical language were vitally necessary to counter allegations of extreme subjectivity and narcissist self absorption. The combination of a dearth of well-qualified dance teachers with an absence of a sense of direction for dance education nearly spelled its death in the state system at this juncture.

It was timely for the resolution of this educational dilemma that it should have coincided with the evolution of Ballet Rambert into a contemporary company in the mid-1960s and with the establishment of the London Contemporary Dance Theatre by the end of the same decade, thus creating an artistic context in which dance education might again begin to thrive.

## The London Contemporary Dance Theatre's Growth in the UK: Its Contribution to a Change in the Educational Parameters of Dance

In a previous study of the London Contemporary Dance Theatre and Ballet Rambert during this crucial period of 1965–1975, I charted some of the significant events in the establishment of both of these companies as "modern" or "contemporary" companies. I also analyzed similarities and differences in their practices (Adshead & Mansfield, 1985; Adshead & Pritchard, 1986).

The first time that British dance-goers could appreciate Martha Graham's work in the theater was in 1954, in London, and in 1963 in London and Edinburgh. Enthused by what he saw, Robin Howard set up the Contemporary Ballet Trust in 1966, which, with Robert Cohan as artistic director, gave its first performances in 1967.[31] The move into The Place in 1969 heralded a more stable existence. The Trust's aims included the provision of "a distinctively British form of contemporary dance" (Robin Howard, *First Real Draft and Submission to Trusts*, 1969). By being "firmly rooted here but international" and "importing the best from overseas to set the standard and provide leadership," it sought to give "the maximum encouragement to young creative and performing artists."

In Howard's view Contemporary Dance was "an attitude" not a technique since "it is concerned with using movement of the human body to communicate something to an audience, and usually something about human beings. Training the body and developing the self will give the artist something to communicate," he argued and this something "must always be developing and changing" (Howard, 1969). But training how? An innocent and naive body is not a real possibility. As Lepecki (1996: 67) argues, choreography "maintains a close relationship with history," to the extent that the "spirit" of a form eludes subsequent reconstructors or translators. There can be no compensation for not being there, in this case during the 1940s and 1950s, when Graham's great and lasting works were conceived. The body is always marked by its experiences and training, and in this sense Howard was naive, and Cohan simply modernist, in their assumption that contemporary dance could release itself from its history and lose its American roots to become "distinctively British."

In recent theorizing of the relationship between art and culture, Helen funded with Local Education Authorities, which began in 1980. In one of a number of pilot schemes[34] the company adopted a residency model which required a dance artist to teach over several weeks and the company to develop new choreography in open rehearsal. Free booklets were provided, supported by various business and charitable organizations including the National Westminster Bank. This much more systematic approach grew into residencies over longer periods of time, the first, for example, in 1976 in Yorkshire which culminated in the première of Cohan's *Khamsin.*

Another typical residency model was the Hampshire project which lasted for four weeks, involving four secondary schools. It was funded jointly by the Arts Council, Southern Arts Association and Hampshire Education Authority (Tobin, 1985). The first week was a public showcase for the company and gave young people an opportunity to see something of the size and scope of its activities. This was followed by a period in which two dancers and musicians worked with students to create a performance. Care was taken to prepare both teachers and students for the work, although there was never sufficient time or money to do this adequately and misunderstandings between artists and educators arose (Briginshaw, 1983; Cole, 1993). Tensions between standards appropriate for the professional company and for education, and between company priorities and educational commitments, were always a problem for the London Contemporary Dance Theatre as for all dance companies.[35] The success of such projects was heavily dependent on the company providing a liaison officer who had some knowledge of the educational world and in this respect the LCDT's Richard Mansfield was exemplary.

Teachers expressed a need for support of the kind that companies could not provide, for example, in the teaching of dance appreciation, and in developing students' own choreography, an alien concept which revealed an interesting distinction between the concerns of the professional dance school and the dance education program in the school sector. Dancers felt more comfortable in technique sessions than in creative classes and neither group felt sure of what could be expected or demanded in this new venture. While dancers might be trained to dance they were rarely trained to teach. Conversely, teachers were constrained by the emphasis on creativity in teaching at the expense of knowledge and skill in dance, the position inherited from the teacher education system described earlier. Although the work was augmented by the creation of resources in video and written forms, for example, by the National Resource Centre for Dance with a video and pack of Cohan's *Hunter of Angels* in 1984, these instances were exceptions rather than the rule.[36]

Free tuition, residency work and days at the theater became readily available in the cities to which the company toured. In his 1985 report

Mansfield claimed that 17 000 young people had benefited from this activity since 1983 (Tobin, 1985: 90). A number of other initiatives sprang from this development and groups of former students worked as Teaching Teams, culminating in *The London Contemporary Dance Experience* in 1983.

As a consequence of these educational developments, the London Contemporary Dance Theatre's own choreography (notably that of Robert Cohan) was seen more widely, new choreography was encouraged, and there was a strong temptation for insecure dance teachers to adopt the School's teaching methods whether or not these were appropriate given the different aims of the school system.

Barely had these projects been established, however, than the political necessities of the 1980s ensured that arts funding was spread more widely across regions, across dance styles, and across cultural and ethnic groups. This is another example of the quite extraordinary compression of the time scale for development and establishment of new initiatives, in all walks of life, in the second half of the twentieth century. It reinforces the argument of the unusually rapid rise and fall of modern dance in the UK and underlines the strange irony of its timing in the face of changing priorities in the cultural context of the arts.

## Contemporary Dance in Miniature: Emulating the LCDT

The success of the London Contemporary Dance Theatre (Clarke & Crisp, 1989) and its School led to a boom in dance activity and to the formation of a number of small companies in the UK. This period shared with the American model the spawning of many small companies often closely linked to educational institutions. Between 1972 and 1982, some 110 companies across the UK were active in disseminating the message of Contemporary Dance to a wider public, filling the smaller venues where the London Contemporary Dance Theatre had started, but for which it had now grown too large (Davies, 1985). Accessibility to wider audiences was the focus and, in the desire to appeal to new spectators, the dances created for this purpose moved a long way from the Graham-based repertoire that was evident in the first years of the company.

An early example of the London Contemporary Dance Theatre's educational impact can be seen in the birth of Spiral Dance Company, started in 1976 by Irene Dilks (an LCDS graduate who also lectured in higher education) to give performances locally, mainly in secondary schools. The company picked up the methods adopted by the London Contemporary Dance Theatre offering workshops and classes based on technique and on repertoire. Interestingly, for what lay ahead, their first paid director was Timothy Lamford who, although trained at LCDS, also had connections with X6 and the emergent "new" dance movement.

EMMA (East Midlands Movement Association), under the direction of Gideon Avrahami (ex Ballet Rambert) with choreography by Tamara McLorg, among others, was active from 1977, and offered: "a two-hour programme of dance consisting of four or five dance works in different styles ranging from the serious to the light-hearted"; a session labeled "Introduction to dance" for younger audiences; a "Choreographic demonstration" lasting one-and-a-half hours and a "Class/Workshop" of the same duration giving practical work under the tuition of a member of the company.[37] This is entirely typical of the period and such activity was replicated across England (and to some extent Wales and Scotland). The effect was substantial since the ten Regional Arts Associations, which by then had considerable budgets, were in a position to fund these companies. An infrastructure developed within which this activity could take place, linking the Regional Arts Association and Local Authority funding structures to educational institutions at secondary and higher education levels.[38]

With even greater relevance to education some companies pursued these objectives very directly by setting up as Dance in Education Companies as, for example, did Ludus, a parallel to the rather better developed Theatre in Education initiatives. Thus just as the splintering of a centralized theater force, the London Contemporary Dance Theatre, spread Contemporary Dance into the regions so, too, the educational work spread, carried forward by these small companies. Consequently, to the disadvantage perhaps of the originators, it became cheaper and easier to support the policy of regionalization of the arts, and to promote local developments in education in this way rather than to work with national companies.

## Paradoxical Dancing Positions

The decline in audiences for modern/contemporary dance was a cause of concern by the time of Devlin's report to the Arts Council in 1989. As early as 1982, Clive Barnes was addressing the question of how it was possible to continue to remain "modern" beyond the thirty years of modern dance's existence. In the USA, despite its "vibrant, athletic dancing," he found evidence of its death throes in the loss of an "explosive creative energy"; in its popular but banal forms; in its "strong infusion of chic, not counterbalanced by a strong infusion of style" (Barnes, 1982: 31), in its repeated worn out formulae of Expressionism. An echo of these concerns is found in Macaulay's review of the LCDT 1983 season in the UK under the title "More or Less Contemporary," in which he asks where the dance is in what he argues is simply an evocation of immaculate technique. This becomes a perennial refrain during the late 1980s. Macaulay, in particular, begins to sound rather peevish about it, saying that the company is "stuck in a rut" in which nothing significant happens (1983; 1987). The London Contemporary Dance Theatre has become London Contemporary POP Theatre, and London Contemporary CHARM Theatre in his blisteringly dismissive tirades. Neither Cohan's archetypes, Bannerman's anonymity, Jobe's facile entertainment, nor Davies's "with-it moodiness," as he characterized the new works of the season, satisfied Macaulay.

Percival (1983) offers a different explanation connected neither to POP nor to CHARM. He links the two foremost products of the London Contemporary Dance Theatre, Richard Alston and Siobhan Davies, to a move towards the "classical" in their apparent concern with dances about dancing. This is a Cunningham-inspired classicism, not one derived from ballet (although Percival (1983: 16) persists in calling their works "ballets"). An alternative view of what some saw as a trivialization of contemporary dance can be found in the association of this streamlined, body-beautiful company with the fashion houses and with a fading aerobics movement, neither of which was calculated to increase serious modernist dance audiences' commitment.

By 1991 it was the new chief executive of the company who argued that the LCDT should "find choreographers who offer us red-blooded choreography that is about emotions and life and relationships, as opposed to works that are just about steps" (Goodwin, 1991: 31). The conflict between two worlds is nowhere more evident than in Noel Goodwin's characterization of the problem: "better a theatrical statement, however lop-sided, than the mimsy, time-serving, inward-looking movements to which so much 'modern' or 'post-modern' dance has tended" (p. 31). At this time, as Artistic Directors came and went with alarming rapidity, the London Contemporary Dance Theatre's lack of direction was marked.

This is still an issue. Celebrating Rambert Dance Company's seventieth birthday in 1996, the tensions were again highlighted between pluralism, often bringing with it enhanced audience appeal and adherence to a modernist vision of greater unity. In an article which bemoaned the absence of new choreographers, Christopher Cook (1996) found more to praise in the revival of Tudor's *Dark Elegies* for its re-animation of the past, than in its new works. During the same summer season John Drummond's view of Rambert's programming was even less complimentary ("vulgarly inept," was his expression; Drummond, 1996: 12) although he elevated Cohan's *Stabat Mater* as "a deeply considered dance classic" (p. 10). Drummond recalls with nostalgia the early years of the London Contemporary Dance Theatre, Robert Cohan's drive, the fifty-nine works he created between 1954 and 1989, forty-three of which were danced by the London Contemporary Dance Theatre. This is an achievement that cannot be taken away from the man, the company or the school. It seems to me to be less than convincing, however, to attribute the downfall of the company to personality problems between the apparent heirs to his monumental construction, as Drummond does. Instead, an understanding of the changing pattern of artistic concerns in the postmodern world, combined with a lack of appreciation of what might be achieved with a repertory-based modern dance company prepared to revive its best works, may provide a more satisfactory account.

## Back at the (American) Ranch

Meanwhile the peculiarly a-historical timing of these events was becoming evident. The UK was taking on a form which, in its original context, was dying. In North America (or more accurately in New York) postmodernism had already challenged the dominance of modern dance. Banes's record of new art movements from 1962–1964 and her subsequent writing on the Judson Dance Theatre (Banes 1980; 1983) provides evidence of the tensions between dance in large capital cities and the rest of a country. Something similar, it might be suggested, exists between art and education. In both cases a time lag seems inevitable and this is borne out by the events in the UK.

It was twenty years after these major challenges in North America before modern dance in its American form became well established in the UK. Perhaps something of this sensibility influenced the eventual choice of title for the London company of "Contemporary" dance. Like those other American virtues of motherhood and apple pie, no objection could be raised. Who would not want to be contemporary? In pressing its claim to relevance in modern British society of the early 1970s, the London Contemporary Dance Theatre avoided the larger question of whose culture it represented and whose history it commented upon and enshrined. It assumed, falsely, that North American and European history and culture were essentially the same.

Extemporary Dance Theatre's history makes interesting reading in this conflict of dance styles. Initially an offshoot of the London Contemporary Dance School, it established itself as one of the most successful small modern dance companies between 1975 and 1981, performing frequently in university and college venues.[39] It was the first of the new smaller contemporary dance touring companies to achieve middle-scale status.[40] It commissioned work from some of the well-known London Contemporary Dance Theatre names of the period, such as Richard Alston and Micha Bergese, but also encouraged its own members and graduates from a number of schools to make new work, for example, Corinne Bougaard, Jonathan Burrows, Tom Jobe, Timothy Lamford, Tamara McLorg, and Janet Smith.

Under Emilyn Claid (its director from 1981 to 1988) it changed its character and developed two distinct roles, sitting uncomfortably on the fence between Modern Dance and "New" Dance. Its roles were both that of a repertoire company and of an experimental, project-based group. In the latter guise it drew on works by Emilyn Claid, Katie Duck, David Gordon and Lloyd Newson – none of whom owed a great deal to London Contemporary Dance Theatre – while in the former it retained evidence of its attachment to the company.

## The British New Dance

The changes being brought about by the British contributors could be seen in embryo in a number of new initiatives which all began around 1977 and 1978. In 1977 the Association of Dance and Mime Artists held its first festival giving a new group of performers a public platform. While some sprang from the early success of the London Contemporary Dance School's training program, many came from a different direction altogether as, for example, did Rosemary Butcher, Emilyn Claid and the X6 Collective.[41]

The American, Mary Fulkerson's initiative at Dartington College was seen in a series of Festivals held from 1978 at which many US postmodern artists appeared for the first time in the UK, signaling interests closer to the Judson Dance Theatre than to Martha Graham's modern dance. Such performers as Katherine Litz, Steve Paxton and Nancy Udow joined a band of British experimenters, now enlarged with the addition of Laurie Booth, Miranda Tufnell, Sue MacLennan and others.[42]

The puzzlement that these changes evoked can be read in the literature of the time. A review of a late Dartington International Dance Festival in 1985, when it was in its seventh year, explores the difficulty of distinguishing between experimental *theater* of the 1960s and this new form of *dance* (or is it movement?). Katie Duck's *Orange Man* was described as full of "inconsequential happenings" with silly, childish and disconnected events competing for attention until Steve Paxton's intervention. Paxton "shook loosely and wildly for about 10 minutes while Group O occupied other parts of the floor". Saddler concludes that it was both exciting and incomprehensible (Saddler, 1985: 11).

A new journal, *New Dance*, began life in 1977 explicitly "by, for, and about dancers". In this emerging field, it emphasized commitment to feminism, political activism, and personal involvement through its collectivist policy and its closeness to dancers and choreographers. It set itself up in direct contradiction to the mainstream critical establishment. What was shared among otherwise very different performers was a desire to challenge the traditional hierarchies of both ballet training and Graham-based contemporary dance. Company management typical of ballet companies had by then been taken on by modern dance companies, if not to the same extent. Similarly, these performers shared a critical attitude towards the kinds of male–female relationship in dance which had remained largely undisturbed throughout the century in ballet and which had barely been disrupted by modern dance.

When *New Dance* reflected on its existence ten years later at a celebratory conference, Fergus Early stated that what it stood for was "liberation . . . of women . . . of dancers" from economic oppression by funding bodies; of black people; "of the individual, to make and perform dance"; from "dictatorial patterns of learning" (Early, 1987: 10). In particular he highlighted the contributions of Richard Alston, Jackie Lansley, Sally Potter, Christopher Banner and Wendy Levett who, between them, brought film, visual art and martial arts to dance. This eclecticism, combined with a political agenda, served to distinguish new dance quite strongly from both the modernism of contemporary dance and from the so-called "postmodernism" of many of the Judson choreographers.

Dance Umbrella, the festival of performance of new dance which began in 1978, also made claims for dance styles other than the American or European modern dance. During its heyday of presenting experimental work (a role now taken over to some extent by "Resolutions and Evolutions" seasons at The Place and later, spring loaded, and new work at the ICA) the same names recur: Alston, Butcher, Claid, Dupres, Early, Smith, Spink, Tufnell. Interestingly, however, links with other British art worlds of theater, film-making, sculpture and minimalist art were already evident, again moving the focus of interest from American to European interests. From 1972, Richard Alston's works were performed as often in art galleries as in conventional theater spaces. He continued to create small-scale work at the same time that the London Contemporary Dance Theatre was expanding to fill the Sadler's Wells Theatre. By contrast, Rosemary Butcher never straddled this uncomfortable divide and devoted herself exclusively to the development of new movement-based work in quite different venues. Royal Ballet choreographers and dancers such as Ashley Page also joined these experimental events, while Mime artists, Butoh performers, South Asian dancers and musicians, and many other diverse groups brought a richness of cultural heritage into relationship with Release and Contact-based work from the North American postmodern movement.

## Britain in Europe: Some Conclusions

Significantly, while the London Contemporary Dance Theatre was busily establishing its audiences and extending its education work, the dance world was beginning to move on. Reflecting the shifting ground in North

America, but more focused on Europe, attention turned to work which had the potential to comment upon political and social issues, on gender identity and, within dance, on the use of hierarchical training systems to oppress dancers. The original democratic ideals of the early modern dance movement had been lost in the codification of both the technique and the development of company structures. Greenberg and Levin's modernism, already challenging what had previously been more Expressionist in character, had moved Martha Graham's modern dance aside in favor of the high modernist explorations of Cage, Cunningham and Rauschenberg. Martha Graham was already the doyenne of "historic modern dance" by the mid 1960s.

In another context the British tendency to adopt all things American after the war had also waned. Closer relationships across Europe encouraged a reappraisal of a shared cultural heritage. In the early 1960s the agreement to form a European Common Market (European Union) was the culmination of a return to this older cultural heritage; as World War II was retreating into memory a new generation perceived the historical necessity of understanding a shared if conflicted past. It signaled the end of the post-war dependency on North America, in art as in politics, in education as in life, in dance modernism as in postmodernism.

In a recent and topical article the art historian Marcia Pointon discusses the role of the new Tate Gallery for modern art at London's Bankside. Acknowledging that "British" is a synthetic term used deliberately as a unifying concept, she argues that the new gallery should embrace the "contradictory cultural fragments of a past in which differences . . . are paramount". If the label "British" is sometimes used to defy foreign competition, it is also useful in locating a relationship with the wider Europe. In a parallel that is a direct rehearsal of the debate for dance, she argues that "it is time to acknowledge that a North American-inspired, modernist internationalism has little relevance to the historical study of European art," and suggests that "it is time to embrace the paradox – that British art exists but that it can only be recognised through the diversity of a European context . . . to be European, we must recognise ourselves culturally as British; and to be British, we must acknowledge ourselves culturally as European" (Pointon, 1997).

This is revealing in relation to the paradox of the rise and fall of the London Contemporary Dance Theatre from the 1960s through to the 1980s. The London Contemporary Dance Theatre's inheritance carried the North American modernist burden of trying to create new, abstract Expressionistic and a-historical work. It did so in an era which became highly self-conscious about its historical debt and when interest had moved from the USA to Europe. This refusal to be colonized, which might be seen as a rather nice reversal of roles, in retribution for the original British colonization of the USA, can perhaps be attributed to a longer cultural history for Britain in the melting pot of Europe. The British seem not to feel the need for the kind of national imaginative identity that Anderson (1991) attributes to Americans. At some level, they are unsympathetic to such ambitions.

At the beginning of this article I suggested that changes in the education system in the late 1960s and early 1970s in the UK coincided with an equally crucial shift in forms of dance. The effect was the rise to eminence of an American form of modern dance, an abstract Expressionist form. In its turn, while it suited the mood of the time and offered dance education a new lease of life tied to a new understanding and appreciation of modern art, it was a valedictory echo of an earlier period. Its day had passed; and at its height it was gradually replaced by a breadth of dance and movement forms that answered more directly to the cultural pluralism and artistic diversity of the late twentieth-century postmodernist world of Europe.

The importance of the London Contemporary Dance Theatre in revitalizing both theater dance and dance education should be recognized, and its demise understood in the context explored above.

## *References*

Adshead, J. (1980) Dance as a discipline. Ph.D. thesis, University of Leeds; subsequently published in part as *The Study of Dance*, 1981. London: Dance Books.

Adshead, J. and Mansfield, R. (1985) *London Contemporary Dance Theatre 1967–1975*. University of Surrey: National Resource Centre for Dance.

Adshead, J. and Pritchard, J. (198) *Ballet Rambert 1965–1975*. University of Surrey: National Resource Centre for Dance.

Anderson, B. (1983 [1991]) *Imagined Communities: Reflections on the Origin and spread of Nationalism*. London: Verso

Arts Council of Great Britain (1978–1979) *Annual Report*. London: Arts Council of Great Britain.

Banes, S. (1980), 1987 *Terpsichore in Sneakers*. Boston: Houghton Mifflin.

Banes, S. (1983) *Democracy's Body. Judson Dance Theatre 1962–1964*. Durham: Duke University Press.

Barnes, C. (1982) Modern dance: has it a future? *Dance and Dancers*, October, 31–33.

Briginshaw, V. (1983) The Dance Artist in Education in Great Britain 1945–1982. Unpublished M.Phil. thesis, University of Leeds.

Best, D. (1974) *Expression in Movement and the Arts*. London: Lepus.

Best, D. (1978) *Philosophy and Human Movement*. London: Allen & Unwin.

Best, D. (1985) *Feeling and Reason in the Arts*. London: Allen and Unwin. Reworked and published 1992 as *The Rationality of Feeling*. Brighton: Falmer.

Brinson, P. and Dick, F. (1996) *Fit to Dance*. London: Gulbenkian Foundation.

Brooke. J.L. and Whiting, H.T.A. (eds) (1973) *Human Movement: A Field of Study*. London: Kimpton.

Clarke, M and Crisp, C. (1989) *London Contemporary Dance Theatre*. London: Dance Books.

Cole, A. (1993) Partnerships: Dance Artists in Education. Unpublished Ph.D. thesis, University of Surrey.

Cook, C. (1996) The ties that bind. Rambert's 70th birthday party. *Dance Theatre Journal*, 13, 6–7.

Coton, A.V. (1975) *Writings on Dance 1938–68*. London: Dance Books.

Daly, A. (1995) *Done into Dance*. Bloomington, Indiana: Indiana University Press.

Davies, S. (1985) Shifts in patterns of funding for Small-Scale Dance Companies, 1976–1981. Unpublished M.A. Dissertation, City University London.

DES (1972) Teacher education and training. Report of the James enquiry. London: HMSO

Devlin, G. (1989) *Stepping Forward*. London: ACGB.

Drummond, J. (1996) A golden stage. *Dance Theatre Journal*, 13(2), 10–12.

Early, F. (1987) Liberation notes. *New Dance*, 40, 10–12.

Franko, M. (1995) *Dancing Modernism/Performing Politics*. Bloomington: Indiana University Press.

Goodwin, N. (1991) London Contemporary. *Dance and Dancers*, January, 31–32.

Grove, L. (1895) *Dancing*. London: Longmans.

Gulbenkian Foundation (1980) *Dance Education and Training*. London: Gulbenkian Foundation.

Gulbenkian Foundation (1982) *The Arts in Schools. Principles, Practice and Provision*. London: Gulbenkian Foundation.

Hirst, P. (1973) Liberal education and the nature of knowledge. In *The Philosophy of Education* edited by R.S. Peters, pp. 87–111. London: OUP.

Hodgson, J. and Preston-Dunlop, V. (1990) *Rudolf Laban· An Introduction to His Work and Influence*. Plymouth: Northcote.

Howard, R. (1969) *First Real Draft and Submission to Trusts*. London: LCDT Archive, The Place.

Jordan, S. (1992) *Striding Out Aspects of Contemporary and New Dance in Britain*. London: Dance Books.

Kennedy, D. (1964) *English Folk Dancing. Today and Yesterday*. London: Bell.

Laban, R. (1947) *Effort*. London: Macdonald & Evans.

Laban, R. (1948) *Modern Educational Dance*. London: Macdonald & Evans.

Laban, R. (1960) *Mastery of Movement*. London: Macdonald & Evans.

Layson, J. (1970) The contribution of modern dance to education. Unpublished M.Ed. thesis, Manchester University

Layson, J. (1987) Isadora Duncan: her life, work and contribution to Western Theatre Dance. Unpublished Ph.D. thesis, University of Leeds.

Lepecki, A. (1996) How modern is modernism? *Ballet Intenational/tanz Aktuell*, 8/9, 67–69.

Macaulay, A. (1983) More or less contemporary. *Dancing Times*, January, 277–279.

Macaulay, A. (1987) LCDT dancing LCDT choreography. *Dancing Times*, January, 306–308.

Manning, S. (1993) *Ecstasy and the Demon: Feminism and Nationalism in the Dances of Mary Wigman*. Los Angeles: UCLA.

Odenthal, J. (1996) Contemporary dance needs, and will find, an historical perspective. *Ballet International/Tanz Aktuell*, October, 33–35.

Odom, S. (1991) Dalcroze Eurhythmics in England: history of an innovation in music and movement education. Unpublished Ph.D. thesis, University of Surrey.

Percival, J. (1983) Two of a kind. Siobhan Davies and Richard Alston. *Dance and Dancers*, April, 14–17.

Pointon, M. (1997) *The Times Higher*, 3 January: 15.

Prestidge, M. (1987) Dartington – The Dance Festival. 1978–1987. *New Dance*, 40, April–June, 18–19.

Preston-Dunlop, V. (1963) *A Handbook for Modern Educational Dance*. London: Macdonald & Evans.

Pritchard, J. (compiler) (1996) *Rambert. A Celebration. The First Seventy Years*. London: Rambert Dance Company.

Redfern, H.B. (1973) *Concepts in Modern Educational Dance*. London: Kimpton.

26. Added to Best's earlier texts (1974, 1978) were early versions of chapters of his subsequent 1985 book for example in the *British Journal of Aesthetics*, the *British Journal of Educational Studies*, *The Journal of Aesthetic Education*, *Philosophy*, the *Journal of Human Movement Studies* – all of which were readily available to teacher educators.

27. His 1985 text was reworked and republished in 1992. Chapter 12 exposes the fallacies of much thinking on the subject.

28. While all histories can be said to share certain concerns each is different in its questions and develops methods which respond directly to different activities.

29. Smith-Autard's attempts to disguise these problems by reference to a "mid-way model" between educational and professional worlds of dance reveal instead conceptual confusion and an a-historical view of dance in education (Smith-Autard, 1994). The "art" of dance is simply tautological and makes no sense unless one can substitute something else for the word "art." It is simply a plea for value since nothing else will fit.

30. A recent national report, "Fit to dance" by Brinson & Dick (1996) underlines the importance of these issues in the face of a rise in injury to dancers. This report emphasizes the close relationship between athletes and artists in this most physical form of art.

31. Histories of this period and the evolution of contemporary dance can be found in White's (1985) *Twentieth Century Dance in Britain*, written by Mansfield for London Contemporary Dance Theatre, and Pritchard for Ballet Rambert.

32. Tetley gave Ballet Rambert six works in a short period of time. He was, however, already more closely involved with European dance than Cohan, in extending his work to the Netherlands.

33. Again the impact of this over time can be seen in the development of similar ventures by established British dancer/educators inspired by the example of the London Contemporary Dance School, e.g. at Thamesdown Dance Sudios with Marie McCluskey and at Harehills School in Leeds, with Nadine Senior. The latter subsequently evolved a new further education program at the Northern School of Contemporary Dance, which in its turn has recently become a degree course, validated by the University of Leeds.

34. The scheme was widened within a few years to include artists and companies from other cultural traditions including Indian and African-related initiatives before it ended in 1985.

35. The residency model was one that had flourished in North America enabling modern dance to create new audiences in universities, to recruit dancers from performance-based dance programs and to acquire rehearsal space. Many American college dance programs stem from these initiatives of Graham and Humphrey (among others). Modern dance is still the predominant form taught in many dance programs in higher education in the USA but the rationale for its introduction shows an interesting discontinuity with the British scene. In the absence of a thorough-going dance education program in schools, the introduction of modern dance into higher education in the USA served aspirations to create new audiences as well as to provide dancers for new small regional companies. The role of dance within the education program of the USA was, and remains, quite different from that in the UK.

36. This work subsequently became a set work for GCE school examinations, which in itself indicates the extent to which modern dance of this kind had become both respected in the theatre and valued within education.

37. Program material from the period.

38. Anne Cole (1993) traces these developments and constructs an educational case for work with artists.

39. Archive materials held in the National Resource Centre for Dance, University of Surrey.

40. These are categories used for Arts Council funding purposes. This implied stability and gave a guarantee of a future.

41. See Jordan (1992) for further discussion and records of the activity during this period in England.
42. A short article summarizing the achievements after ten years can be found in Prestidge (1987).

Figure 13
The London Contemporary Dance Theatre in *Cell*. Choreography, Robert Cohan.
Photo: Anthony Crickmay. Courtesy of V&A Picture Library.

think that is what they wanted to destroy and they succeeded in destroying it. A lot went with it.

RM: This family feeling or connection became quite widespread, beyond those employed by the organization. It became a sort of network across the country. After work with the LCDT, when I had a company in the north of England, I found people in Yorkshire and Durham who somehow felt that they had a piece or a place in that family. There are still some of them around. This talk of a family brings us back to the mysterious way Robin used the word "love."

JE: Yes, Robin used that word all the time. It embarrassed the later board, not the original board which had people who understood it. People like Irene Worth and Lord Harwood and Gielgud. As we went along they were replaced by businessmen, so when Robin started talking about love they thought, "what is he talking about?" They had not a clue what he was on about. There were times when he would cry a bit in board meetings because he was upset or worried or frustrated. They could not envisage what this was about, but it came from his heart.

So I remember those words in the Arts Council appraisal: "It's time the organization is no longer run as a family." That was, I think, the biggest mistake.

RM: Yes, perhaps the opposite objective would have been better. It should have continued to run as a family and the franchise of that family should have been extended. Of course animosities arise within families.

JE: Yes, but then in a crisis that animosity is not there. There was a great deal of jealously in the outside world towards the company. Robin was not a yes man to the Arts Council and they did not like that. He was not always popular. He would fight for things; he was awkward. So when all his money was gone . . . well.

RM: Can we talk a bit about Robin, the school and training or education?

JE: Robin felt it was very important to develop the mind as well as the body. That is why, in those early years, he made sure he had fascinating people in this building. It was not just dancers. We had the Royal Shakespeare Company, we had the Fires of London. We had exciting people around us. The board of governors in those years were personalities. Then, as time went on, the board became people who might help us raise money or marketing people. It was a very different group of people. Robin was an individualist. He was not a corporate man. He found himself quite trapped.

RM: I talked to Sean Feldman about something in the school called "Robin's course."

JE: He tried to allow the students to really be themselves. He was very frustrated with the school towards the end because he felt it had all become far too academic.

RM: Academic in the sense of a concentration on reading and writing?

JE: Yes. He felt people were getting bogged down with this and that they were not allowed to be themselves. He felt they could not express themselves as they really wanted to.

RM: Talking to us when we were young dancers, Robin used the word "love" as it is used in religious terminology, meaning something like accepting a positive attitude to the world as a wonderful mystery. The use of such words in this way gets pushed away by the business world and by the academic world. Both feel they must speak in precise terms and can't deal with what can't be put into words.

JE: But dance is not about words. Robin felt you can express yourself without words and that everyone should have that opportunity. Beyond that, he felt a great need for a more humane approach to the students. He also felt there needed to be a new way of training.

RM: In dance training now there seem two ways that what is important gets squeezed out. First, through becoming too academic in the fairly traditional sense of the word "academic," and second through the dance technical demands becoming more important than their purpose.

RM: Robin instigated degree-based qualifications as a basis of the training within the London School of Contemporary Dance. He brought in a principal for the school who had an academic background to initiate and see to that instigation.

JE: He felt that we had to go down that road because people who had twenty years of experience, and were obviously very good teachers, could not get jobs because they did not have a piece of paper. On the other hand, people who had a piece of paper, who had never danced in their lives, were getting jobs. He felt the best teachers were those who had danced as professionals. He was shocked that people were teaching who had never danced professionally. There were those who had been wonderful professional dancers, and were excellent teachers, but could not get the job in a university. So, he felt we should give that opportunity to the professionals.

RM: This was a degree for people who had already been professional dancers, not for students who had not danced professionally yet.

JE: It was to be both, so students could get the degree while training and professionals could get a degree while continuing to dance. But, he felt that it started to get over the top.

RM: There may be some marriage between academic study and professional dance training that can be accomplished or which can be accomplished by some people. But the problem is in . . .

JE: . . . not losing sight of what you are about . . .

RM: . . . because you are talking about dance, or reading about dance, or using a different part of your mind or using your mind in a way you don't use it when you experience dance.

JE: Then Robin was outrageously pushed out of here, destroying the man who made it all possible. He spent the last few months of his life interviewing over forty-five people in the States and he had an equally long list of people to interview in Europe. He felt there was a need to find a new way forward for training. I have all the tapes of him talking to Merce, to Paul, to Alvin Ailey, to Twyla Tharpe, you name it. He spoke to all the Americans. Unfortunately, he died before he got to talk to everybody here. He was going to put it all together.

I tried to transcribe these discussions. It was very hard, but I've got it all. One day I'll find the right thing to do with them.

[*As often happens, talk continued after the tape recorder was turned off. In this case the conversation concerned how something could usefully be published on Robin. Janet mentioned that he had done a great deal before he set up the LCDT and that any book about him ought not to speak only about what he had done in dance. For example, before founding the Contemporary Dance Trust, he had organized the evacuation of refugees from Eastern Europe.* RM]

## Reference

Clarke, M. and Crisp, C. (1987) *The London Contemporary Dance Theatre*. London: Dance Books.

## Note

1. The director of The Place Theatre who has encouraged young experimental choreography there.

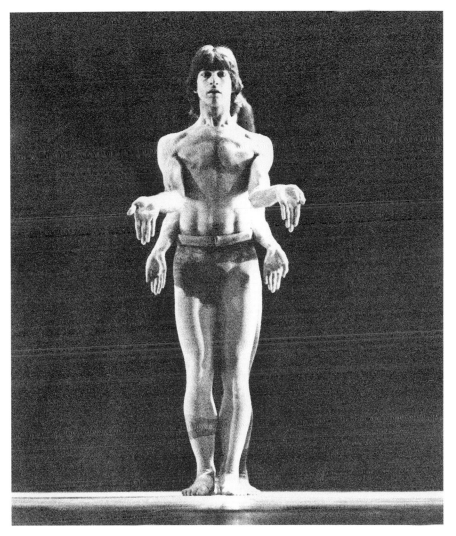

Figure 14
Anthony Van Laast in *Forest*. Choreography, Robert Cohan.
Photo: Anthony Crickmay. Courtesy of V&A Picture Library.

# Awareness, a Life Force and a Kind of Ecstasy: An Interview with Robert Cohan

Ross McKim

At: The Place
On: 8 September 1998

RM: This issue was to be based on the question "Has the London Contemporary Dance Theatre had influence on dance now?" Through earlier interviews it became clear that, of course, there has been such influence, but this might be only because the LCDT was a biggish institution. Also, though people say there has been such influence, they often cannot point to what it is. When they do point to what the "it" is, they speak of things that would probably have come anyway from other sources. So I will ask you what the things were that you did in the LCDT which have influence on dance now? I hope we can arrive at something special that is left, or could be recovered, from the LCDT that is unique and valuable.

RC: There were three motivations for us and the problems which they addressed, although they have been partially solved, have not been totally solved. One motivation was to make available a place for dance to be done, actually performed. Robin [Howard] and I tried to provide the opportunity for anybody to perform. I'm not talking about making a dance in the studio. We can all do that. You can make up a dance in your living room, but not until you perform it is it a fixed work of art. The opening has then been made and something magical takes place. So we wanted to provide a place where anyone could book the theatre and dance. We tried that in the beginning and it didn't work because nobody was trained. So we had a lot of one-nighters at The Place that should not have existed.

I was thinking about the YMHA in New York which you could rent for one hundred dollars for one night. They would do all the publicity, sell the tickets and put you on their announcement. You had one themselves. Not just, I am aware of my arm, but how are you aware of your arm? How detailed can this be? Is it your arm? If you are separate enough from it to be aware of it, is it your arm? Is it something that you are only borrowing for the time being while you are here? All these aspects come when you start to work on physical awareness, which is what dance is about. How can you relate your life to your physical body? How can you bring experience from now and from the past into dance form and, because it's in dance form, see it better and go past it? Can you search into yourself for help, through intuition? Can a teacher open you to yourself? This can be done through making a dance that you have to inhabit, that you have to fill up. It is one of the ways of making you grow and see yourself, of helping or teaching a person to come into his or her own artistic form and artistic shape.

You have to think of life on that basis; a means of becoming aware. Graham did and I am sure it's what Ruth St Denis did for Graham and someone did for Ruth St Denis. Its handed on. Gurdjieff is sideways to all that. Gurdjieff is about that most people are asleep; even most people who think they are awake are asleep. Man's job on earth is to wake up and take responsibility for himself. Most of us are too terrified of that moment of waking up so we just go ahead with our lives as they are. For me, that fitted in very well with what was going on at the Graham studio. To take responsibility for yourself as an artist by trying – I am not saying actually to wake up – but by trying to wake up and become aware.

RM: In thinking about how the LCDT was different I think as much about what went on in the studio as about what went on in performance and of thinking at home about what went on in the studio. Were you conscious of working on "waking up" in the studio?

RC: Yes and no. I would be pretending if I said that I knew how to bring it about. But yes because I knew the moments would come and I knew everybody would recognize them when they came in the studio. How to set things up so that would happen became the problem. There were always moments in the studio, not every day, when everybody knew that everything was right with the world. That's a magic moment and that's an illuminated moment for me. It's a moment when you are not thinking about anything at all and everybody is doing something special at that moment and it's trance-like or hypnotic. You are not out of your mind. You are very aware, but you are in another place. We all recognize when those things happen. Those moments you look for. I looked for them. You try to set up a situation which is just the opposite of learning by rote and just rehearsing the steps. You are looking for something else to happen and this "else" is an illumination. This was, for me, the essential purpose of dance.

It is very unlikely that it would get on the stage, because the stage is such an artificial place and such a difficult place. I have felt that the stage gets the residue of the experience that we had in the studio. Does that make sense?

RM: Yes, it does. I'm trying to grasp what the experience you are talking about is. I can remember during a class of yours thinking, "this is just where I want to be and this is just perfect." We were not, at that point, jumping up and down. It was quite quiet. Later I read Curt Sachs saying all dance is "ecstatic" and thought "oh come on." But there is such experience even in the studio and even in class. Such dance ecstasy is not something out of a Hollywood movie. It can be quite subtle.

RC: I absolutely believe that. After saying it's very hard to achieve on the stage, I should be more specific and say it's hard to achieve it with a group. Personally, however, you can achieve it on the stage. I have vivid memories of moments of performing when everything was right. These are experiences which you would have to describe in very poetic words. People might compare this to drug experience or religious experience, but it was not drug induced. These experiences are not the result of a chemical being produced in the brain to overcome the pain of dancing. They were moments when everything in life is right.

In daily life it's very hard to find equivalent situations. You find it perhaps when you are very emotionally involved, perhaps in love. You might find something similar in a church or cathedral as a kind of exultation. You might feel it in witnessing a sunset or landscape because it is so beautiful. It's not emotional, in the normal sense, like being moved to tears. It's a moment of absolute rightness. It is not an uncommon experience but dance is a wonderful opportunity to create it. You are using physical language which uses the entire body in which you have to coordinate as much of yourself as you are aware of. Not just the head, although the head is involved, but the whole body from your feet to your fingernails. Everything can come together like that especially if you are working in the studio with like-minded people. That consensus can help produce it and help bring it together. I'm not saying you can't get it in other art forms but dance is a very good way of getting it because it is very intense.

It is ecstasy only in reflection. You are in that place that, for me, feels like perfection. By that I mean rightness. That is a kind of ecstasy compared to the rest of your life.

RM: You mentioned consensus. I feel that what happened in the LCDT reflected and was the result of what you, more than anybody else, did and tried to do. Everybody in the company in consensus – I know there were little rebellions – accepted, even if sometimes not knowing it, that they would pursue what you pursued. So I want to pursue now what it was that you pursued.

to disappear in a year or two and those ideas will be thrown away. There will be a new best thing, a nouveau thing rather than something which has significance as an art.

RM: When I came here there was a feeling of being protected that was perhaps lost, forced out, later.

RC: I think that's what happened. I think everybody wanted a piece of the thing and the thing was no longer there for all its pieces being taken. Do you know what I mean?

RM: You mean people outside the group?

RC: Outside the group. So they thought, "here is this successful contemporary company, why not send it to Hull?" We would say, "who in Hull wants to see the LCDT?" Then we would have to go and they would say, "you used to be successful but you only did 100 people a night in Hull. You are not successful anymore." This is the attitude we were facing. Why should we go to Hull without Hull knowing what they were to get? Anyway, what did Hull have for the LCDT? They had all been put out of work because there are no more herring. Maybe two or three hundred people in Hull wanted to see it. So do one night, but we had to play Hull for a week because that was the system. We played mining towns where forty per cent of the town was out of work. Of course the audience didn't come. Nobody had any money. How could they come to the theatre? They could not feed their children. This is the sort of stupid thing that happened. This is what I mean by saying everyone wanted a piece of it. They said we can send the LCDT there and they can fill in this or that date.

RM: When you came over from the States and the Graham company, did you plan to get into this big business thing?

RC: No, not at all. I wanted to dance actually. I thought if I had a company in London I could dance more often. Well that went by the board very fast. I did want to choreograph but what was really attractive was setting it up from nothing, from scratch. We could build a school and a company. There was a building to work in. Robin and I and Mop (Janet Eager) would talk it out so that everything was right. And to a great degree we achieved that for the first five, six, seven maybe eight years. Then it got out of hand because it was too successful. It got too big. We had not planned for success. We thought it would be so difficult to do that we would never succeed.

RM: Robin, in the back of that white book puts a date for it (Clarke & Crisp, 1987: 190). He says 1976, which is very early, was the date at which he ceased to be able to do what he wanted to do.

RC: I went to Robin, I can't remember the exact year. It may have been '78. It may not have been that early. I said, "Robin, this Sadler's Wells season in November should be our final season." He said, "What do you mean by that?" I said, "We will never be better than we are now.

We have all had a wonderful time. We should close the door. We should shut everything down at the end of the season. The empty space that we will leave will cause such an implosion. It will be filled with other people and other things because we have opened so many doors and have been successful. We should close now." And he was so shocked. He said, "I have to sleep on this." Then the next day he said, "I can see what you are saying and I agree it would be the right thing to do, but I could not put that many people out of work."

RM: What would you have done if he had done what you suggested?

RC: I would have been very happy, I think. I would have gone on choreographing. I could teach and choreograph. I would have gone somewhere else, maybe back to the States. I had no plans but it did not scare me to do that, although I had no money. I had no money at all during the entire time of the company because salaries were so minimal for everybody. I hardly got paid for the work. I think I got royalties of three pounds a night for my pieces; maybe I got five pounds.

RM: I remember the residency of 1976. You seemed really rather happy. We were back to eight dancers in a little bus roving around Yorkshire. After a demonstration you said, "I jumped, I haven't jumped for years."

RC: Yes, because that was containable. You had the audience and the work in the palm of your hand. I don't mean we could not perform in the big theatres, we could. That also was containable. But the rat race of those years became uncontainable.

The biggest problem was finding the way financially and otherwise to produce all this new work. We had no money to bring pieces in, so we had to create it all ourselves. You all produced a lot and I did the other fifty per cent.

RM: You were into dancing and being a choreographer, but you were into something else.

RC: That's true, I was working on several things. I was working on myself a lot, trying to make myself more of what a human being can be. As a choreographer I was working on something very specific, which I have talked about to a few friends, but not many. Martha used to say that she was a witness to her dances. I thought, the first time I heard her say that, that it was absolutely right. If you were with her when she created some of those magical works, you knew there was something else operating there. It wasn't Martha as the person Martha, and it wasn't us. It was something else. It was part of what I call this "thing of rightness." The work was being done by another hand through her hand. I tried to do this. I wanted to be like a magnet that energized those around me. I tried to be fully energized. I knew what the idea for the work was. I knew what the quality was, the sensation, the feeling, the taste. I tried not to interfere with that but to let "it" create the dance. I tried to work directly from intuition from inner . . . inner translations. I tried not to intellectualize. I intellectualized later on, looking at the videos or looking at the work the next day, but not during the creative moment in the studio. I think a lot of you knew that was happening. People would say "How do you want me to do it?" I'd say, "I've no idea. I'll tell you when I know." Now I couldn't do that all day, every day without fail. Sometimes I was more successful than others.

RM: This would have taken some preparation and protected studio time. If you are back in the studio having been burned up from being on tour. . . .

RC: That's the problem. You need a great deal of energy to do this. It's not really passive and you can't be weak. You need a great deal of energy to be such a "witness."

You say I was working on something else. I was working on myself. I also was very conscious – maybe this is Gurdjieffian – that if you want to go up a step you have to put someone on the step you are leaving. That's the responsibility of an artist who is a leader. It was selfish, because if I did not put them up, I could not go up.

RM: You pulled people up behind you. But a thought a lot of people have is that when Cohan was not there to lead the LCDT, nobody could. It's said to be a mystery why, with all these wonderful people who were produced, when you left, nobody could take it on.

RC: Yes, because I made my leadership very personal. Not intentionally. I wanted enormously to give other people more responsibility because I thought it would allow me to be more creative. I wanted help. Yes, it didn't work. Maybe it shouldn't. Maybe it can't.

RM: Was the situation not solvable?

RC: It was solvable but only with more money. It's interesting that the Arts Council gave us money in direct proportion to how Robin got poorer.

RM: I have thought that the special atmosphere of the LCDT in the early days had something to do with feeling that Robin could pick up the deficit. Each year something like a Rodin would disappear from his house. Finally there was nothing left.

RC: But that made me guilty of spending his money. I felt the Arts Council should be doing this. We were one of their leading companies. The Arts Council should have taken responsibility for us. There was no fat to be cut. When Thatcher began to cut the fat we had no fat so we were cut.

It is an unanswerable question: what we could have done under another situation. We were forced into an impossible situation. We had to work within it to the best of our ability and there was no lying down on the job. We could have done with some understanding from the funders. They did not understand what we were doing. They were under pressure too. All they could see was the number of bums on seats. They did not look at the work and, if they did, they saw only the last thing you had choreographed.

That was not what it was about. It was about the entire operation, The Place. It was about the school, the atmosphere in the building, the creative feeling, the people that were being produced. It was about the life force that was here.

## Reference

Clarke, M. and Crisp, C. (1987) *The London Contemporary Dance Theatre*. London: Dance Books.
Kandinsky, W. (1977 [1914]) *Concerning the Spiritual in Art*. New York: Dover.

Figure 15
The London Contemporary Dance Theatre in *Diversion of Angels*; Linda Gibbs in the foreground. Choreography, Martha Graham. Photo: Anthony Crickmay. Courtesy of V&A Picture Library.

proportion of both these cases. Medieval cathedral building provides an example. The most important element that informs the appearance of a medieval cathedral is probably the belief that every aspect of that construction has a relation to an overpoweringly meaningful numinous presence. Both the process (the making) and the product (the building once made) are vehicles to something beyond them. As it is true that "unbelievers can enjoy the cathedrals, but we never could have built them" (Fuller, 1980: 190), the later LCDT did not seem able to build dances of the kind the early company had built. This was not because skills had been lost but because state of mind and an attitude towards making dance, and indeed towards the world, had been.

Robin Howard chose Martha Graham-based technique to begin his work on dance art as vehicle. By the time he chose it, this had a foundation in Jungian thought. Jung said transformative experience and knowledge result from bringing into consciousness what is normally unconscious. He said this could be done through art, though he spoke very little about dance. Graham almost certainly experimented with the conviction that dance might work toward what Jung called "individuation". This is the never-ending process of becoming a more enlightened individual. In the Gurdjieffian thought that influenced Robert Cohan's development of Graham's work, such transformative experience and knowledge arise through awaking from a "waking sleep." The experience and knowledge which is so rendered can provide a positive attitude to the world which Howard called "love."

It is unwise to underestimate Robin Howard's understanding of this word or to disregard it as woolly-minded, sentimental romanticism. Bertrand Russell wrote of a ". . . possibility in the human mind of something mysterious as the night wind, deep as the sea, calm as the stars and strong as death . . ." (Russell, 1975 [1969]: 319). Russell called this "a mystic contemplation, the 'intellectual love of God'" (p. 319). He took the term the "intellectual love of God" from Benedict De Spinoza (b. 1642). The latter meant by it a condition that springs from the highest knowledge which is, in fact, beyond intellect as that term is commonly understood. Spinoza says that from the highest form "of knowledge necessarily springs the intellectual love of God. For from this kind of knowledge arises joy" (Spinoza, 1937 [1865]: 274). This knowledge, says Spinoza, comes through seeing the world *sub specie aeternitatis* which can be translated as "under the aspect of eternity." This was to see and understand the world as Spinoza believed God did.[1] The world thus becomes a whole and as it should be. Russell would have said he did not believe in God so, for him, Spinoza's intellectual love of God was a love of the world.

Another advocate of love, whose concept of it was sophisticated, practical and influential during Robin Howard's life was Mohandas

Gandhi. Gandhi recognized contributions to his notion of love to have derived from sources like Christianity[2] and Tolstoy. It stands within his concept of Ahimsa or non-violence. Ghandi says "true Ahimsa should mean a complete freedom from ill will and anger and hate and an over-flowing love for all" (Ghandi, 1983: 207). Ghandi believed Ahimsa, or the practice of the application of love to all the acts of ones life, was a very practical force towards success.

After Ghandi's death his thought was taken up by Martin Luther King, who wrote a book called *The Strength to Love*. He says, "The meaning of love is not to be confused with some sentimental outpouring. Love is something much deeper than emotional bosh" (King, 1986 [1964]: 50). King says, "The greatness of God lies in the fact that he is both tough minded and tender hearted" (p. 15).

Howard's concept of love, which he wished should affect all the process of the Contemporary Dance Trust, might be understood to be on the same level as those of Russell, Spinoza, Ghandi and King. If so understood it was not a sentimental concept, it was not "emotional bosh" nor does it exclude being "tough minded".

The experience and attitude that resulted from Howard's understanding of this concept; it was very likely a source of the LCDT's success. The loss of it was perhaps a major cause of its failures. For a time the LCDT made available, to a network of people, performances that supplied special experience, knowledge and even, for some, something of a consequent attitude to the world. It then ceased to be able to do so. Once Robin's vision of "love" had been lost at the center, the results of working through it could no longer be supplied through performance. While he managed to keep the organization "alternative," it seemed able to make such provision but when it became "mainstream" it could not.

Some of the opposition that would eventually burden the LCDT and sap its creativity was the result of resentment towards its seeming success and its acquisition of a place within this main stream. The weight of this opposition should not be underestimated and it is easy to forget how much of it there was. It is discussed, to a limited extent, in the Janet Eager and Robert Cohan interviews and Janet Adshead-Lansdale's article states some of the arguments of this opposition. She articulates the view that the company failed because it remained American. It failed because ". . . [Howard] was naive, and Cohan simply modernist, in their assumption that Contemporary Dance could . . . lose its American roots to become 'distinctly British'." For Adshead-Lansdale the company's work remained "back at the American ranch". But beyond this she appears to say that, at least often, the LCDT did not even produce good American art: ". . . nothing could be further from the refined aestheticism of the American modernist movement as exemplified by Clement Greenberg via his followers."

Effective opposition to the real objectives of the LCDT were applied from the business and academic worlds once the LCDT became something of an establishment. As the Eager and Cohan interviews say, through the Arts Council the business side of the arts world demanded that the company should make more money. In hindsight, trying to do so appears to have been a fatal act. The academic side of the arts world demanded the organization alter its educational processes if these were to be funded. Howard had wished to bring out the "thinking dancer." Eager says he came to believe that the experience of thinking and putting a certain area of thought into words (writing), had replaced, rather than enhanced, the experience he wished his school to pursue through dance. He seemed aware that the essential experience of dance, like Spinoza's intellectual love of God, might never be entirely grasped by, or acquired through, the intellect. It might have to remain that which "cannot be put into words [but] makes itself manifest [being] what is mystical" (Wittgenstein, 1974 [1921]: 73).

In the sense that Wittgenstein uses the term, Robin Howard and Robert Cohan were very practical men working in a "mystical" tradition. But mystics in the West have had to keep a guarded distance from convention and from conventional business and education. The lesson to be learned from the LCDT perhaps includes how it succeeded when it retained its concern for the mystical (in Wittgenstein's specific sense), why it lost them and what the effect of that loss was.

I am suggesting we experiment with the hypothesis that the LCDT, in its most successful period, worked at dance as vehicle. The vehicle was one in which the objective was to obtain transformative experience that, in turn, might finally render a positive attitude to the world. Through this it may become clear what lies behind what the contributors of this issue have found remarkable about the LCDT.

The Bannerman interview introduces the notion of the work of the LCDT as vehicle. Speaking of the technique the company pursued he says "it is possible to separate certain principles which were being transmitted from the vehicle of transmission, the vehicle being in this instance the Graham based technique." Speaking of the dance making of the company in general he says "for me it was a transformative experience and so dance was a vehicle. I had the sense that this was true for others and for Bob Cohan himself. I also think that he intended at least some of his work to be that . . . [but] at some point this aspect was obscured or even lost".

The question that emerges is to what objective was this dance making a vehicle. Bannerman admits there might be a likeness in the motivations for his first journey to India and his attraction to the LCDT. Both were numinous journeys. Certainly Bannerman believes that for Cohan and for him dance, within the LCDT, had been a vehicle of inner transformation.

He speaks of a "direct relationship between the so called technique taught and a philosophical stance," which he found "very interesting and in fact compelling."

Christopher Bruce speaks of the work of Ballet Rambert of the 1970s as being "compositionally rather amorphous and the dancing, maybe a little undisciplined on occasions." To correct this he looked to "not only the LCDT which was strongly based on Graham, but also the ballet-based Netherlands Dance Theatre." But why was it the case, within the LCDT, that as Robert North says in his interview "a disciplined work ethic was taught but it did not need to be enforced?" This may have been so because the technique of the LCDT emerged out of the art of vehicle frame of mind which had created Modern Dance itself.

Bruce also makes it clear that he has made ballet the basis of his company's work and discipline. This throws up the question of whether ballet technique can validly be the basis of a Contemporary Dance company. Bruce believes it can.[3] Nonetheless, almost all the early Modern Dance creators and many of the Modern and Contemporary Dance creators that followed them would argue that a Modern or Contemporary Dance company requires a Modern or Contemporary Dance technique. A company primarily based on ballet technique is a ballet company. Modern Dancers from Wigman through Humphrey, Graham, Cunningham and others invented new techniques, while the Contemporary Dancers who followed them expanded on these and combined them. They seem to have believed they needed to create their own dance techniques as vehicles.

The reason most Modern and many Contemporary Dance creators have not used Ballet technique as their primary basis may be related to its emphasis on certain inhibitions on the use and experience of the body. They wish to explore the experiential revelations dance can provide as I have discussed in part two of my introduction to this issue. This is an important point as concerns the LCDT. A great deal of the originality of the company arose out of Robert Cohan's studio-based "research" through daily classes, into the possibilities of Contemporary Dance technique as vehicle. Cohan's choreography in itself is important. Yet, beyond this it is difficult to think of any other dance maker of his generation (if he represents a dance generation between Graham, Humphrey, Hawkins and Cunnigham and the younger artists of the present) who has so thoroughly investigated Contemporary Dance technique through "class." He used this investigation to inform the choreographic material of his company. What was distinct and original about the LCDT probably cannot be separated from what was distinct and original about its attitude towards, and how it worked on, a technique particularly appropriate to its own use.

When a Contemporary Dance technique is new, its purpose tends to be understood because it has recently been invented. But it is possible to have a technique-based discipline through a dance technique, the purposes of which are forgotten. In the latter case discipline may be only a meaningless habit. Discussion around this point emerges in the Richard Alston interview. He says the central difference between Rambert Dance Company and the LCDT in Robin Howard's time was not merely a choreographic one, but the result of the technical dance basis of each. He says of the dancers at Rambert, "their skirmishes with Graham work were sort of motley" and that "London Contemporary still retained a different role. There was a kind of weightiness and physicality that was much gutsier, much less pretty than Rambert."

Alston also spoke with some feeling of how the attitude to dance art as vehicle generated not only a particular way of working but also "an enormously organic feeling to this building. Don't you think so? Do you remember that? It was a family." He comments on how this "family" was extended into what he calls an "infrastructure." Then he says "the infrastructure has gone, something has weakened." The article concerning the Northern School of Contemporary Dance testifies to the value and power of this family feeling when it was strong. Members of a family are often held together through the sense that there is something valuable shared between them. In the case of the LCDT family this sense appears to have been justified. What was valuable may have derived from the creation, or support, of dance with a profoundly meaningful purpose.

Sean Feldman speaks of what was instilled through the Contemporary Dance technique as taught at The Place. "Probably the most significant influence on me from that time was the passion Jane [Dudley] put into her teaching . . . ." This passion may be related to Robin Howard's "love." He brought Jane Dudley to teach in his school, not only because she could teach movement skills, though of course she could. Jane, Feldman says, instilled something that carried students beyond technique for its own sake.

Speaking about dance technique Feldman talks of a "depth" within the dance he learned. "Jane and the other teachers I had as a student taught me to move from as deeply within me as I could. The work I do now ('release') also explores movement that comes from deep in the body. So both Graham work and the release-based work move towards developing an expressive and articulate instrument." Cohan pursued the connection between deep muscle use.[4] This connection, now the subject of various forms of physical therapy that are based on "depth" psychology, calls out for a good deal more investigation through dance.

Feldman further comments on the direct influence of Robin Howard on him and other students through "Robin's course." In this course students were made aware that self-expression could be a vehicle.

Howard's course was about "expressing ourselves in whatever way we felt we needed to or was appropriate to us individually and as a group." By then, apparently frustrated by his school, Howard, Feldman says, "was mainly concerned that the course offered us as much support for our own personal development as people, not just as dancers, as possible."

Feldman also speaks of his experience working with Siobhan Davies, one of the most important of present British choreographers. It can certainly be argued that Davies' humane attitude to her dancers has some relation to her experience as one of the first generation of students at the London School of Contemporary Dance and to her experience as a dancer and choreographer with the LCDT. Feldman speaks of how Davies is concerned that "when we are working that we take care of ourselves. If you're injured Sue will check to see that you are getting the treatment you need." Speaking of how Davies "embraces" that her dancer colleagues have a life beyond the studio and the stage. Feldman speaks of how she "encourages the dancers who've had babies to come back when they are ready."

In my time in the LCDT Robert North was perhaps the most rebellious member. Yet he was probably, at foundation level, of one mind with Cohan and Howard. This is brought out in his interview, in which he says "I thought 'you can change yourself'." North's attitude contained, not a difference of essence, but what he calls "a difference of emphasis." In agreement with Cohan and Howard he says "You should work on something that has something profound about it and not just something superficial." Asked if he thought dancers could work, through dance, on their "deeper selves", he says "I made fun of it but I think I thought that was right."

Importantly North makes the point, not made elsewhere in this issue, that the dance of the LCDT is not the only kind that might function as art as vehicle. Often it was perhaps not even what is commonly called dance. His interview brings to mind that, if transformative experience is available through dance, there must be different kinds of it, just as there are quite different kinds of dance.

When asked about the "slick company" the LCDT became, Janet Eager said quietly but firmly "that was probably not where Robin's heart was." Something essential was made most clear in her interview. Howard was emphatic that his not unsophisticated conception of "love," as both vehicle and object of that vehicle, should be embraced by his professional dancers, his students and even by his board of management. It also reveals the extent to which the later Contemporary Trust board, the Arts Council and even finally, in his view at least, Howard's own school were unable to grasp this basis of the organization. The Contemporary Dance Trust, through its board, would eventually dispense with Robin Howard, its creator. The Arts Council attacked and demanded the elimination of the "family" quality of the organization which arose naturally out of Howard's convictions and on which depended much of its creativity. Academic respectability, Janet Eager says, caused Robin to become "very frustrated with the school towards the end because he felt it had all become far too academic."

Howard spent the last days of his life interviewing the most creative dance artists of the time towards evolving a new form of dance training. Eager says "he felt there needed to be a new way of training." Eager reports that this training would, Howard said, be informed by "a great need for a more humane approach to the students."

Something of the specific way in which the dance-making work of the LCDT was art as vehicle is clarified in the Robert Cohan interview. First he speaks of the "dance artist" which Robin wished to create. Cohan says such people, through their dance "live in a special world . . . it has different rules and different laws." He speaks of the possibility of personal change through dance, citing the thought of Gurdjieff and how this informs a notion that one can "wake up" through dance.

Cohan tried to set up situations, in his company, in which everyone experienced that "everything was right with the world." Asked about the nature of the experience of individual dancers at such moments he says, "It is ecstasy only in reflection, because you are in that place that feels like perfection, by which I mean rightness. It is a kind of ecstasy compared to the rest of your life." He relates this to Howard's concept of love saying, "Well we finally had to come to a definition of love. It was, in the end I think, this feeling of rightness." "A feeling of rightness" very nearly describes the world when viewed *sub specie aeternitatis*, as I discussed above. It sustains Spinoza's and Russell's "intellectual love."

Cohan allowed his dancers to experience that they were "in another place. . . . Those are the moments you look for. You try to set up a situation that is just the opposite of learning by rote and just rehearsing the steps. . . . You are looking for something else to happen and this 'else' is an illumination." Cohan wished that his company members should be "going through a process of growth" in which the vehicle of growth was the process of making and performing dance and the process of preparing to do those things.

The LCDT was probably not essentially about making successful performances, though this followed during the period when it retained its purpose beyond them. As Cohan says there remains "an unanswerable question [of] what we could have done under another situation." The situation that killed resulted from lack of understanding. Those who came to control the LCDT, from within and from without, did not understand what had made it successful. These people Cohan says "did not understand what we were doing . . . they saw only the last thing you had choreographed." He says: "That was not what it was about. It was about the entire operation. It was about the school, the atmosphere in the building, the creative feeling, the people that were being produced. It was about the life force that was here." This "life-force" seems co-equal with what Robin Howard called "love." The processes and products of the LCDT, in its best days, were a vehicle towards the experience and expression of this life force or this love.

## References

Fuller, P. (1980) *Beyond the Crisis in Art*, London: Writers and Readers Publishing Co-operative.
Ghandi, M. (1983) *The Essential Gandhi*. New York: Vintage Books
King, M, L. (1986 [1964]) *Strength to Love*. Glasgow: Fount Books.
Russell, B. (1975 [1969]) *Autobiography*. London: Unwin.
Spinoza, B. (1937 [c. 1865]) *Ethic*. London: Oxford University Press.
Wolford, L and Schechner, R. (1997) *The Grotowski Sourcebook*. New York: Routledge.
Wittgenstein, L. (1974 [1921]) *Tractatus Logico-Philosophicus*. London: Routledge and Kegan Paul.

## Notes

1. Spinoza's notion of God was unconventional. He said "By God I understand being absolutely infinite" (Spinoza, 1937 [1865]: 274).
2. So Christ says "This is my commandment, that ye love one another, as I have loved you" (John 15: 12).
3. He states in his interview, however, that he supplements ballet training with Modern Dance training and particularly Cunningham-based training.
4. This is also discussed in the Robert North interview, this issue.

Figure 16
The London Contemporary Dance Theatre in *Stages*. Choreography, Robert Cohan.
Photo: Anthony Crickmay. Courtesy of V&A Picture Library.

# The LCDT Repertoire

Jane Pritchard

| Date | Work | Choreographer | Composer[1] | Designer[2] | Last year |
|------|------|---------------|-------------|-------------|-----------|
| 10/10/67 | *Piece for Metronome and Three Dancers* | Patrick Steede | | | 1967 |
| 10/10/67 | *Eclipse* | Robert Cohan | Eugene Lester | Charter,[3] John B. Read (l) | 1979 |
| 10/10/67 | *Sky* | Robert Cohan | Eugene Lester | Peter Farmer (d) (1971) | |
| 10/10/67 | *Witness of Innocence* | David Earle | Grazyna Bacowicz | Michael Robinson | 1967 |
| 10/10/67 | *Family of Man* | Anna Mittelholzer | Judith Knight | Projections by Charles Dunlop | 1967 |
| 10/10/67 | *Hunter of Angels* | Robert Cohan | Bruno Maderna | Walter Martin (c), John B. Read (l) | 1979? |
| 10/10/67 | *Tzaikerk* | Robert Cohan | Alan Hovhaness | Brian Benn (l) | |
| 02/09/69 | *Side Scene* | Robert Cohan | | Noberto Chiesa | 1969 |
| 02/09/69 | *El Penitente* | Martha Graham | Louis Horst | Isamu Noguchi reproduced by Peter Donohoe, Jean Rosenthal (l) | 1971 |
| 04/09/69 | *Hermit Songs* | Alvin Ailey | Samuel Barber | | 1970 |
| 04/09/69 | *Cortege* | Barry Moreland | Johann Sebastian Bach | | 1968 |
| 04/09/69 | *Shanta Quintet* | Robert Cohan | John Mayer | | 1969 |
| 09/09/60 | *Hosannas* | Barry Moreland | Domenico Scarlatti | Richard Armstrong | 1970 |
| 09/09/69 | *Reef* | Patricia Christopher | Ted Dockstader | | 1969 |
| 11/09/69 | *Solo and Trio for Two* | Clover Roope | Alexander Goehr | | 1969 |
| 11/09/69 | *Cell* | Robert Cohan | Ronald Lloyd | Noberto Chiesa (s), Charter (c), John B. Read (l) | 1994 |
| 29/04/70 | *Gourami* | Jack Nightingale | Traditional Japanese | Francine Daniells | 1970 |
| 29/04/70 | *Raga Shankara* | Flora Cushman | Clem Alford, Keshav Sathe | | 1972 |

| Date | Work | Choreographer | Composer[1] | Designer[2] | Last year |
|------|------|---------------|-------------|-------------|-----------|
| 29/04/70 | *Something to Do* | Richard Alston | Gertrude Stein (words) | | |
| 29/04/70 | *Divertissement in the Playground of the Zodiac* | William Louther | George Quincey | Peter Docherty (s), William Louther (c) | 1971 |
| 28/05/70 | *Three Epitaphs* | Paul Taylor | American folk | Robert Rauschenberg (c), Jennifer Tipton (l) | 1985 |
| 29/05/70 | *Conversation Piece* | Robert North | Michael Parsons | Peter Farmer (d) | 1971 |
| 31/05/70 | *Vesalii Icones* | William Louther | Peter Maxwell Davies | John B. Read (l) | 1970 |
| 31/05/70 | *Nocturnal Dances* | Barry Moreland | Peter Maxwell Davies | John Gunter | |
| 04/06/70 | *Duet* | Paul Taylor | Joseph Hayden | George Tacit | |
| 24/07/70 | *X* | Robert Cohan | Mauricio Kagel | Peter Farmer (d) | 1970 |
| 13/10/70 | *Rainmakers* | Pauline de Groot | Floris Rommerts | Pauline de Groot | 1970 |
| 15/10/70 | *Summer Games* | Barry Moreland | Samuel Barber | Peter Donohoe | 1970 |
| 23/10/70 | *Streams* | Robert Cohan | Alan Hovhaness | Peter Farmer (d) | 1970 |
| 30/12/70 | *Cantabile* | Noemi Lapzeson | Michael Finnissy | Peter Farmer (d), John B. Read (l) | 1978 |
| 06/01/71 | *Nowhere Slowly* | Richard Alston | Terry Riley | Nora Stapleton (l) | 1971 |
| 07/01/71 | *Macroseconds* | Flora Cushman | | Flora Cushman (l) | 1971 |
| 13/01/71 | *The Consolation of the Rising moon* | Robert Cohan | John Williams | Peter Farmer (d) | 1972 |
| 27/01/71 | *The Troubadors* | Barry Moreland | Peter Maxwell Davis | Barry Moreland (s), Jenny Henry (c) | 1971 |
| 03/02/71 | *The Road of Phoebe Snow* | Talley Beatty | Duke Ellington, Billy Strayhorn | Jenny Henry (c) | 1972 |
| 21/04/71 | *Stages* | Robert Cohan | Arne Nordheim, Bob Downes | Peter Farmer (d), Anthony McCall (Film), John B. Read (l) | 1974 |
| 25/01/72 | *Scenes from the Music of Charles Ives* | Anna Sokolow | Charles Ives | Peter Donohoe (masks), Jenny Henry (c) | 1973 |
| 27/01/72 | *One was the Other* | Noemi Lapzeson, Robert North | Michael Finnissy, Bob Downes | Noberto Chiesa (d), John B. Read (l) | 1972 |
| 27/01/72 | *Some Dream* | Xenia Hribar | Antonio Vivaldi, Tomaso Giovanni Albioni | Jane Hyland (c) | 1972 |
| 01/02/72 | *Cold* | Richard Alston | Adolphe Adam | John B. Read (l) | 1972 |
| 01/02/72 | *Kontakion* | Barry Moreland | Renaisance Spanish Mediaeval | Barry Moreland | 1972 |
| 16/03/72 | *Outshoulder Vision* | Flora Cushman | | | 1972 |

| Date | Work | Choreographer | Composer[1] | Designer[2] | Last year |
|------|------|---------------|-------------|-------------|-----------|
| 16/03/72 | *Brecknocks* | Kurt Dreyer | | | 1972 |
| 11/05/72 | *Dance* | Remy Charlip | (No sound track or musical score. The dancers spoke and sang.) | Charter (l) | 1972 |
| 30/05/72 | *Combines* | Richard Alston | Franz Schubert, Johann Sebastian Bach, Frederic Chopin | Diana Davies (c) | 1972 |
| 30/05/72 | *Scalene Sequence* | Flora Cushman | Milislav Kabelac, Luciano Berio | | 1972 |
| 16/08/72 | *Cunundrum* | Noemi Lapzeson | | Noemi Lapzeson | 1972 |
| 16/08/72 | *Gamma Garden* | Flora Cushman | Shusha, Ignatius Temba | | 1972 |
| 18/08/72 | *Fugue* | Stephen Barker | Robert North | Stephen Barker | 1972 |
| 18/08/72 | *Tearful History* | Ross McKim | Kevin Nutty, Ross McKim | Ross McKim | 1972 |
| 18/08/72 | *Treeo* | Xenia Hribar | Alistair Leonard | | 1972 |
| 29/08/72 | *People Alone* | Robert Cohan | Bob Downes | Noberto Chiesa (s), Jane Hyland (c), John B. Read (l) | |
| 29/08/72 | *Relay* | Siobhan Davies | Colin Wood, Bernard Watson | | 1972 |
| 30/08/72 | *Outside In* | Micha Bergese, Anthony Van Laast | John Lansdown, Alan Sutcliffe | Micha Bergese, Anthony Van Laast | 1972 |
| 12/10/72 | *Brian* | Robert North | Michael Finnissy, John Dodson (text) | Peter Owen (d), Sally Potter (slides), Ian Irving (l) | 1972 |
| 18/12/72 | *Tiger Balm* | Richard Alston | Anna Lockwood | Charles Paton (l) | |
| 18/12/72 | *Dance Energies* | May O'Donnell | Ray Green, Roger Briant | Charter (c) | 1973 |
| 30/12/72 | *Ends and Odds* | Lotte Goslar | | Lotte Goslar | |
| 26/02/73 | *People Together* | Robert Cohan | Bob Downes | Noberto Chiesa (d), Charter (c), John B Read (l) | |
| 03/04/73 | *Mass* | Robert Cohan | Vladimir Rodzianko (1973), Judith Wier (1974) | Noberto Chiesa (s), Charter (c), John B. Read (l) | |
| 07/02/74 | *Pilot* | Siobhan Davies | Igg Welthy, Stephen Barker | Charter (l) | |
| 07/02/74 | *Dressed to Kill* | Robert North | Harry Miller, Dennis Smith | Peter Farmer (d) | 1974 |
| 26/02/74 | *Blue Schubert Fragments* | Richard Alston | Franz Schubert | Michael Alston (l) | |
| 26/02/74 | *Steps of Silence* | Anna Sokolow | Anatole Veru | | 1974 |

| Date | Work | Choreographer | Composer[1] | Designer[2] | Last year |
|------|------|---------------|-------------|-------------|-----------|
| 27/02/74 | *Mad River* | Remy Charlip | Johann Sebastian Bach, Anatol Vieru, Jules Massenet, Peter Ilich Tchaikovsky | Bill Gibb (c) | 1974 |
| 28/03/74 | *Diversion of Angels* | Martha Graham | Noman Dello Joio | Martha Graham (c), Isamu Noguchi (d), Jean Rosenthal (l) | 1975 |
| 11/06/74 | *Waterless Method of Swimming Instruction* | Robert Cohan | Bob Downes | Ian Murray Clark | 1981 |
| 26/09/74 revised 31/02/90 | *Changing Your Mind* | Dan Wagoner | First section danced to the sound of one of the dancers reading a newspaper; second section danced to woodlands sounds. | Charter (l, 1974) Tom Johnson (l,.1990) | |
| 26/09/74 | *The Calm* | Siobhan Davies | Geoffrey Burgon | Charter (l) | |
| 03/10/74 | *Troy Game* | Robert North | Batucada, Bob Downes | Peter Farmer (c), Charter (l) | 1989 |
| 13/11/74 | *No Man's Land* | Robert Cohan | Barry Guy | Peter Farmer (d), Richard Caswell (l) | 1986 |
| 18/02/75 | *Hinterland* | Micha Bergese | Kraftwork, Golden Seve, Andrew Sisters | Bettina Bergese (d), Charter (l) | |
| 18/02/75 | *Still Life* | Robert North | Bob Downes | Peter Farmer (d), John B Read (l) | |
| 20/02/75 | *Masque of Separation* | Robert Cohan | Burt Alcantara | Noberto Chiesa (d) John B. Read (l) | 1981 |
| 24/02/75 | *Extinction* | Cathy Lewis | Tangerine Dream | | |
| 04/06/75 | *Class* | Robert Cohan | Jon Keiliehor (1975), Geoffrey Burgon (1980) | Charter (d), John B. Read (l) | 1988 |
| 29/09/75 | *Stabat Mater* | Robert Cohan | Antonio Vivaldi | Charter (d), John B. Read (l) | 1988 (1994) |
| 06/10/75 | *Diary 2* | Siobhan Davies | Gregory Rose (1975), Morris Pert (1976) | Charter (l) | 1980 |
| 06/10/75 | *David and Goliath* | Robert North, Wayne Sleep | Carl Davis | Peter Farmer (d), John B. Read (l) | 1976 |
| 15/11/75 | *Da Capo al Fine* | Micha Bergese | Dominic Muldowney | Bettina Bergese (d), Charter (l) | 1976 |
| 15/11/75 | *Headlong* | Richard Alston | Anna Lockwood | Charles Paton (l) | |

| Date | Work | Choreographer | Composer[1] | Designer[2] | Last year |
|------|------|---------------|-------------|-------------|-----------|
| 28/11/75 | *Glady, Badly, Madly, Sadly* | Robert North, Lynn Seymour | Carl Davis | Charter (l) | 1975 |
| 22/12/75 | *Place of Change* | Robert Cohan | Arnold Schoenberg | Charter (d), John B Read (l)1981 | |
| 15/01/76 | *The Bronze* | Namron | Bob Downes | Bettina Bergese (d), Charter (l) | |
| 22/03/76 | *Khamsin* | Robert Cohan | Bob Downes | Noberto Chiesa (d), Charter (l) | 1982 |
| 22/06/76 | *Nympheas* | Robert Cohan | Claude Debussy | Noberto Chiesa (d), John B.Read (l) | 1983 |
| 04/11/76 | *Nema* | Micha Bergesse | Eberhard Schoener | Bettina Bergese (d), David Hersey (l) | 1977 |
| 04/11/76 | *Step at a Time* | Siobhan Davies | Geoffrey Burgon | Michael Creevy (Photography), Charter (l) | 1979 |
| 05/04/77 | *Night Watch* | Micha Bergese, Robert Cohan, Siobhan Davies, Robert North | Bob Downes | Noberto Chiesa (d), Charter (l) | 1977 |
| 07/04/77 | *Meeting and Parting* | Robert North | Howard Blake | Peter Farmer (d), David Hersey (l) | |
| 12/04/77 | *Harmonica Breakdown* | Jane Dudley | Sonny Terry, Oh Red | (Tom Johnson) | 1992 |
| 12/04/77 | *Forest* | Robert Cohan | Brian Hodgson | Noberto Chiesa (d), Charter (l) | 1991 |
| 03/09/77 | *Continuum* | Micha Bergese | Morris Pert | Noberto Chiesa (d), John B. Read (l) | 1978 |
| 18/10/77 | *Sphinx* | Siobhan Davies | Barington Pheloung | Charter (l) | 1980 |
| 24/11/77 | *Valse a deux, Valse a six* | Isadora Duncan staged by Madeleine Lytton | Franz Schubert | | 1977 |
| 24/11/77 | *Les Filles du Chalcis* | Isadora Duncan staged by Madeleine Lytton | Christoph Willibald von Gluck | | 1977 |
| 24/11/77 | *Polonaise* | Ted Shawn staged by Norman Walker | Edward MacDowell | | 1977 |
| 08/12/77 | *Rainbow Bandit* | Richard Alston | Charles Amirkhanian | Anne Guyon (c) Charter (l) | 1986 |
| 23/01/78 | *When Summer's Breath* | Micha Bergese | Michael Finnissy | Bettina Bergese (d), John B. Read (l) | |
| 23/02/78 | *Scriabin Preludes and Studies* | Robert North | Alexander Scriabin | Peter Farmer (d), Francis Reid (l) | 1979 |
| 20/04/78 | *Just Before* | Anthony van Laast | 'organized by Anthony van Laast' | Angela Hawkins Charter (l) | |

| Date | Work | Choreographer | Composer[1] | Designer[2] | Last year |
|------|------|---------------|-------------|-------------|-----------|
| 24/04/78 | *Aurora* | Anca Frankenhaeuser | Marcus West | | |
| 24/04/78 | *9-5* | Tom Jobe | John Lewis | Paul Dart (d) | 1978 |
| 08/05/78 | *Box* | Micha Bergese | William Albright | John B. Read (l) | 1979 |
| 18/05/78 | *Falling Man Solo* | Robert Cohan | Barrington Pheloung | | |
| 03/10/78 | *Eos* | Robert Cohan | Barry Guy | Barney Wan (d), John B. Read (l) | 1981 |
| 05/10/78 | *Dreams with Silences* | Robert North | Brahms | Noberto Chiesa (d), John B. Read (l) | 1980 |
| 24/10/78 | *Solo Ride* | Micha Bergese | Douglas Gould | Liz da Costa | 1980 |
| 24/10/78 | *Then You Can Only Sing* | Siobhan Davies | Judyth Knight | Jenny Henry (c), Charter (l) | 1980 |
| 05/12/78 | *Ice* | Robert Cohan | Morton Subotnick | Noberto Chiesa (d), John B. Read (l) | 1979 |
| 29/3/79 | *Treading* | Christopher Bannerman | Daniel Easterbrook | | |
| 02/05/79 | *Kisses Remembered* | Cathy Lewis | Carl Vine | Stuart MacLaine Charter (l) | 1979 |
| 02/05/79 | *Days Untold* | Patrick Harding-Irmer | Joanne Pooley | Charter (l) | |
| 22/05/79 | *Dance for Four* | Tom Jobe | Johann Sebastian Bach | Charter (l) | |
| 22/05/79 | *Scene Shift* | Micha Bergese | Carl Vine | Liz da Costa, John B. Read (l) | 1980 |
| 22/05/79 | *Three Solos* | Linda Gibbs | Dudley James | Adrian Dightam (l) | 1980 |
| 25/05/79 | *Reflections* | Robert North | Howard Blake | Charter (l) | 1980 |
| 29/05/79 | *Sand Steps* | Christopher Bannerman | Marcus West | Jenny Henry (c), Adrian Dightam (l) | |
| 29/05/79 | *Through Blue* | Anthony van Laast | Bruce Cole | Charter (l) | 1979 |
| 07/08/79 | *The Annunciation* | Robert North | Howard Blake | John B. Read (l) | 1988 |
| 07/08/79 | *Songs, Lamentations and Praises* | Robert Cohan | Geoffrey Burgon | Noberto Chiesa (d), John B. Read (l) | 1989 |
| 02/10/79 | *Five Circular Studies* | Robert North | Christopher Benstead | John B. Read (l) | 1979 |
| 02/10/79 | *Ley Line* | Siobhan Davies | Vincent Brown | Craig Givens | 1979 |
| 02/10/79 | *Rondo* | Robert Cohan | John Herbert McDowell | Barney Wan | 1979 |
| 04/12/79 | *Cloven Kingdom* | Paul Taylor reconstructed by Linda Kent | Arcangelo Coralli, Henry Cowell, Edmund McDowell | John Rawlings, Scott Barrie, Jennifer Tipton recreated by Tom Johnson (l) | 1991 |

| Date | Work | Choreographer | Composer[1] | Designer[2] | Last year |
|------|------|---------------|-------------|-------------|-----------|
| 12/02/80 | *One* | Tom Jobe | Bernie Holland | Derek Jarman, Charter (l) | 1980 |
| 12/02/80 | *Some Dance and Some Duet* | Micha Bergesse | Igor Stravinsky | Liz da Costa (d), Adrian Dightam (l) | 1980 |
| 12/02/80 | *Death and the Maiden* | Robert North | Franz Schubert | Robert North (d), Adrian Dightam (l) | 1983 |
| 12/02/80 | *Field* | Robert Cohan | Brian Hodgson | Penny King, Charter | 1980 |
| 07/10/80 | *The Singing* | Christopher Bannerman | Barrington Pheloung | Francis & Chisholm (s), Bannerman, Boughton (c), Charter (l) | 1981 |
| 09/10/80 | *Something to Tell* | Siobhan Davies | Benjamin Britten | Anthony McDonald (d), Peter Mumford (l) | 1981 |
| 18/11/80 | *If my complaints could passions move* | Siobhan Davies | Benjamin Britten | Peter Mumford (l) | 1980 |
| 03/02/81 | *Songs and Dances* | Robert North | Franz Schubert | Andrew Storer (d), John B. Read (l) | 1986 |
| 06/05/81 | *Aspect* | Patrick Harding-Irmer | Caroline Thompson, Barrington Pheloung, Andrew Webster | Tom Johnson (l) | |
| 13/05/81 | *The Homerun* | Philip Taylor | Christopher Benstead | Philip Taylor, Tom Johnson (l) | 1982 |
| 13/05/81 | *Recall* | Jayne Lee | Cathy Lewis | Judy Stedman (d), Charlie Peacock (l) | 1982 |
| 13/05/81 | *Beyond the Law* | Darshan Singh Bhuller | Jon Keliehor | Tom Johnson (l) | 1982 |
| 13/05/81 | *Danger, Work in Progress* | Christopher Bannerman, Eleanor Alberga, Philip Taylor, Darshan Singh Bhuller | Erik Satie, Wolfgang Amadeus Mozart, Stevie Wonder, Glenn Miller, Richard Atree, Eleanor Alberga | Mark Brunet (l) | 1981 |
| 31/08/81 | *Dances of Love and Death* | Robert Cohan | Carl Davis, Conlon Nancarrow | Noberto Chiesa (d), John B Read (l) | 1983 |
| 15/10/81 | *Free Setting* | Siobhan Davies | Michael Finnissy | David Buckland, Peter Mumford (l) | 1984 |
| 04/02/82 | *The Brood* | Richard Kuch | Pierre Henry | Francois Barbeau (d), Mark Brunet (l) | |
| 02/08/82 | *Liquid Assets* | Tom Jobe | Conlon Nancarrow | Tom Johnson (l) | 1986 |
| 14/09/82 | *Esplanade* | Paul Taylor set by Eileen Cropley | Johann Sebastian Bach | John Rawlings (c), Jennifer Tipton (l) | 1985 |

| Date | Work | Choreographer | Composer[1] | Designer[2] | Last year |
|------|------|---------------|----------|----------|-----------|
| 16/09/82 | *Chamber Dances* | Robert Cohan | Geoffrey Burgeon | Noberto Chiesa (d), John B. Read (l) | 1983 |
| 11/10/82 | *Second Turning* | Christopher Bannerman | Gyorgy Ligeti | Anthony MacDonald (d), Charter (l) | 1983 |
| 08/02/83 | *The Dancing Department* | Siobhan Davies | Johann Sebastian Bach, Barrington Pheloung | David Buckland (design and photography), Peter Mumford (l) | 1985 |
| 20/09/83 | *Under the Same Sun* | Darshan Singh Bhuller | John Miller, Clem Alford | Celeste Dandeker(c), Tom Johnson (l) | 1983 |
| 22/09/83 | *Run Like Thunder* | Tom Jobe | Barrington Pheloung | Paul Dart (d), Peter Mumford (l) | 1987 |
| 20/10/83 | *Canso Trobar* | Christopher Bannerman | Martin Best, Barrington Pheloung | Antony McDonald (d), Mark Henderson (l) | 1984 |
| 06/12/83 | *Carnival* | Siobhan Davies | Camille Saint Saens | David Buckland, Antony McDonald (d), Peter Mumford (l) | 1984 |
| 14/02/84 | *New Galileo* | Siobhan Davies | John Adams | David Buckland, Peter Mumford (d, l) | 1985 |
| 16/02/84 | *Agora* | Robert Cohan | Johann Sebastian Bach | Noberto Chiesa (d), Mark Henderson (l) | 1985 |
| 19/09/84 | *Skyward (Skylark)* | Robert Cohan | Eleanor Alberga | Noberto Chiesa (d), John B. Read (l) | 1985 |
| 21/09/84 | *Rite Electrik* | Tom Jobe | Barrington Pheloung | Paul Dart (c), Peter Mumford (l) | 1985 |
| 27/11/84 | *Doublework* | Richard Alston | James Fulkerson | Jenny Henry (c), Peter Mumford (l0 | 1985 |
| 07/02/85 | *Bridge the Distance* | Siobhan Davies | Benjamin Britten | David Buckland, Peter Morgan (d), Peter Mumford (l) | 1986 |
| 24/09/85 | *Moves* | Jerome Robbins staged by Tom Abbott | (danced in silence) | Jennifer Tipton (l) | 1987 |
| 24/09/85 | *Shadows in the Sun* | Christopher Bannerman | Frank Bridge | Andrew Storer (d), Mark Henderson (l) | 1986 |
| 12/02/86 | *The Run to Earth* | Siobhan Davies | Brian Eno | David Buckland, Russell Mills (d), Peter Mumford (l) | 1986 |
| 14/02/86 | *Ceremony/ Slow Dance on a Burial Ground* | Robert Cohan | Stephen Montague | Noberto Chiesa (s), Audrey Gie (c), Charter (l) | 1987 |
| 27/08/86 | *Video Life* | Robert Cohan | Barry Guy | Noberto Chiesa (d), Charter (l) | 1987 |

| Date | Work | Choreographer | Composer[1] | Designer[2] | Last year |
|------|------|---------------|-------------|-------------|-----------|
| 24/09/86 | *Interrogations* | Robert Cohan | Barrington Pheloung | Antonio Largarto (d), John B. Read (l) | 1987 |
| 24/09/86 | *Unfolding Field* | Christopher Bannerman | Man Jumping | Andrew Storer (d), Mark Henderson (l) | 1987 |
| 25/11/86 | *And they do* | Siobhan Davies | Michael Nyman | David Buckland (d), Peter Mumford (l) | 1988 |
| 17/02/87 | *Irma Vep* | Daniel Ezralow | Bela Bartok | Daniel Ezralow, Mark Henderson (l) | 1987 |
| 19/02/87 | *Red Steps* | Siobhan Davies | John Adams | Hugh O'Donnell, Charter (l) | 1988 |
| 24/02/87 | *John Somebody* | Rosalind Newman | Scott Johnson | Antony McDonald (c), Peter Mumford (l) | |
| 25/04/87 | *Hang Up* | Jonathan Lunn | Anthony Minghella (text) | Tom Johnson (l) | 1992 |
| 30/06/87 | *Fabrications* | Robert North | Simon Rogers | David and Elizabeth Emanuel (c), Andrew Storer (l) | 1988 |
| 29/09/87 | *The Pantasmagoria* | Robert Cohan, Tom Jobe, Darshan Singh Bhuller | Barrington Pheloung | Nadine Baylis (d), Graham Large (l and speical effects) | 1987 |
| 1987 | *The Smouldering Suit* | Darshan Singh Bhuller | | Nadine Baylis (c) | 1991 |
| 01/12/87 | *Maybe Tomorrow* | Christopher Bannerman, Paul Chamberlain | Man Jumping | Colin Winslow, Peter Mumford (l) | 1988 |
| 11/02/88 | *Three Dances for Trois Gnossiennes* | Christopher Bannerman | Erik Satie | Tom Johnson (l) | 1988 |
| 11/02/88 | *Bottom's Dream Exquisite Corpse* | Jonathan Lunn | Wolfgang Amadeus Mozart | Tim Reed, Robert Cohan (l) | 1989 |
| 11/02/88 | *Stand by Your Man* | Aletta Collins | Tammy Wynette | Tina MacHugh (l) | 1989 |
| 26/02/88 | *Giant Steps* | Darshan Singh Buller | Dave Heath | Vanessa Clegg, Robert Cohan (l) | 1988 |
| 06/04/88 | *Shift* | Jonathan Lunn | | Jenny Henry (c) Tina MacHugh (l) | 1988 |
| 08/04/88 | *Interlock* | Darshan Singh Buller | Clem Alford | Darshan Singh Buller | 1991 |
| 22/11/88 | *Arden Court* | Paul Taylor | William Boyce | Gene Moore (d), Jennifer Tipton (l) | 1990 |
| 29/11/88 | *Good Morning Monsieur* | Daniel Larrieu | | Mark Betty, Robert Cohan (l) | 1988 |
| 18/04/89 | *In Memory* | Robert Cohan | Hans Werner Henze | Peter Farmer (d), John B. Read (l) | 1989 |

Figure 17
Linda Gibbs, Robert North in *Death and the Maiden*. Choreography, Robert North.
Photo: Anthony Crickmay. Courtesy of V&A Picture Library.

# Notes on Contributors

**Janet Adshead-Lansdale** is Professor of Dance Studies and was Head of the School of Performing Arts (1997–2001) at the University of Surrey. She has written four books on dance history and theory, the most recent being *Dancing Texts: Intertextuality in Interpretation* (1999). She is a member of the Arts and Humanities Research Board (UK) and a member of the Board of Directors of the Society of Dance History Scholars.

**Richard Alston** was among the first intake of students at the London School of Contemporary Dance. He soon established himself as an innovative choreographer making a body of work for the London Contemporary Dance Theatre before setting up his own company, Strider, in 1972. He is now Artistic Director of the Richard Alston Dance Company and of The Place.

**Christopher Bannerman** trained at the National Ballet School of Canada and danced with The National Ballet of Canada and the London Contemporary Dance Theatre. He also choreographed a number of works for the latter. Professor Bannerman has been the Head of Dance at Middlesex University and a Chairman of Dance UK. He is now Head of MA Choreography, MA Choreography with Performing Arts and Head of Rescen (Research Centre) at Middlesex University.

**Alison Beckett,** M.Ed. is Vice Principal (Academic) of the Northern School of Contemporary Dance in Leeds. She joined the College when it opened in 1985 as a lecturer in classical ballet and academic studies. In 1990 she became Vice Principal and was responsible for developing the Bachelor of Performing Arts (Dance) and for curriculum and course development throughout the college. She also acts as a consultant for the development of Higher Education courses in professional dance training and is a member of the Dance Panel at the University of Leeds. Employed as a subject reviewer by the Quality Assurance Agency for Higher Education, she has been involved in reviews of dance provision in both the maintained and private sector.

**Christopher Bruce CBE** trained at the Rambert School. He then danced with Rambert Dance Company. He choreographed his first work for

Rambert in 1969 and his choreography has been central to the company's artistic life ever since. He became Associate Director of Rambert Dance Company in 1974 and that company's Director in 1994. He has choreographed for many major dance companies across the world.

**Robert Cohan CBE** trained with Martha Graham and then danced with her company for over twenty years. In 1966, when he was Associate Director of the Martha Graham Dance Company, he accepted Robin Howard's offer to become Director of what was to become the London Contemporary Dance Theatre. He took charge of the company for another period of some twenty years. He was Director, Chief Choreographer and Teacher of the company. He continues to teach, lecture and choreograph.

**Janet Eager MBE** was engaged by Robin Howard in 1964 at the very beginning of the life of the Contemporary Dance Trust. During the whole of its history she was its Chief Administrator. She was the confidante and advisor to Howard and Cohan during all of that period.

**Sean Feldman** trained at the London School of Contemporary Dance. A uniquely gifted dancer he is particularly known for his work with the companies of Siobhan Davies and Janet Smith. He teaches a sensitive but highly physical brand of Release Technique all over the world. He has choreographed for a number of Contemporary Dance companies.

**Ross McKim** trained at the Royal Ballet School and the National Ballet School of Canada. He danced for the National Ballet of Canada (for whom he choreographed his first professional work), The Royal Danish Ballet and the London Contemporary Dance Theatre (for whom he also choreographed and taught) before forming his own company, Moving Visions (English Dance Theatre). He is now Artistic and Course Director of Rambert School. He has an MA (University of Surrey – Dance Studies) and a PhD (University of Durham – Theology).

**Robert North** trained at the Royal Ballet School and the London School of Contemporary Dance. He danced with Martha Graham and then for fourteen years with the London Contemporary Dance Theatre. He was given the title of Associate Choreographer while with that company. He became director of Ballet Rambert in 1981. In 1986 North moved on to direct several companies in Europe while also working as guest choreographer with major institutions including the Royal Danish Ballet. His latest Directorship has been that of Scottish Ballet.

**Jane Pritchard** is a dance company archivist, historian and author. She established the Contemporary Dance Trust Archive (now at the theatre Museum, Victoria and Albert Museum) and is Archivist for Rambert Dance Company and English National Ballet. She has curated exhibitions on Les Ballets 1933 and presents seasons of dance films.

Figure 18
Robert Cohan, Noami Lapzeson, Robert Powell rehearsing *Sky*. Choreography,
Robert Cohan. Photo: Anthony Crickmay. Courtesy of V&A Picture Library.